Barriers to the Drain:
How to
Make Better Decisions
and Stop Making Excuses

by Robert H. Steffen

Copyright © 2020 by Robert H. Steffen

Barriers to the Brain:
How to Make Better Decisions
and Stop Making Excuses

All rights reserved.
Printed in the United States of America.

At first glance, making a decision and making an excuse might seem to be on opposite ends of the spectrum. After all, we're either going to make a decision, or make an excuse, right?

Looking further, though, we can see that they are actually tied together. Excuses are often what whittle down our choices so that our eventual decisions are arrived at by default - stemming from the elimination of possibilities and opportunities.
With that in mind, *our ability to make quality decisions is incredibly inhibited by the excuses that we use* in the process, the majority of which are created not by conscious thought, but presented to us by our subconscious.

Once we understand the mechanisms in place that lead to these excuses and why they are there, we can devise methods to not only unravel their limiting power, but ultimately use them to our advantage. Take this book for example.
You're either going to read this, or come up with a laundry list of excuses why you aren't - to the point that you'll convince yourself 110% that NOT reading it was a good choice, a right choice, and the best thing for you.

You are *that* good.... *at making excuses*.
That's why we need to get to the bottom of it!

Now, it's human nature to ask "Why?", with a "How?" followed closely behind. We typically don't blindly believe what we're told until we have enough of our "Why"s and "How"s answered satisfactorily. At some point in our lives, we all begin to question why things happen, and why they don't. Nature abhors a vacuum, just as people have a need to find answers and bring closure to the various "Why"s and "How"s in their life.
Naturally, in addition to searching within ourselves and what we know, we look to see what others have filled the gaps of their understanding with. Most of us will gravitate toward those who we can find agreement with and tend to follow who we think have it figured out the best. We adopt those and similar beliefs until we find someone or something else that has answers that sound better, promise more, and/or resonates with what we already believe or want to be true.

My goal is to bring enough explanation to the table
so that whatever suggestions are served up,
you'll find yourself saying "That makes sense".

Because too much information and not enough information are
both great excuses that you've probably used before,
I've tried not to bog you down with too much detail and
information, because I know that "Information Constipation" IS a
thing, and it tends to keep us overthinking and underachieving.
The good news is that, if you do feel the need to know more
about any particular topic or point, we live in a world where
ability and access to additional information is available to all.

My goal initially was to put together a quick, short, easy to read
and understand book that would help you stop making excuses,
which would lead to making better decisions.
It seemed like a simple task.
After all, we all know what excuses are, right?
Yet it's not so much *What* they are that's important, but the
How and **Why** over our lifetime that impacts us the most.

What began as a guide to help you stop making excuses in your
life began to evolve into a work that could transform nearly
every area of your life. That's HUGE. It's also probably more
than you bargained for when you picked up this book.
So, I'm not going to make that claim. You can decide later.
Besides, neither one of us needs that kind of pressure, right?
Let's just focus on why we're here – right now.

Keep in mind, no matter what, everything I'm about to share
here is tied to either the why and the how excuses are made, or
to the drastic reduction of them in your life. YOU WILL NOT
eliminate excuses in your life, and anyone making that promise
is blowing sunshine up your skirt, as they say. If you breathe,
you will still have it in you to make excuses. Period. However,
the underlying mechanisms that would create them will be within
your control to contain. Also, your awareness and recognition of
them will prevent the excuses that do make it to the surface
from having the control over you that they have in the past.
Rather than the mountains they have been before, they will
appear as speedbumps at best.
Did I mention this could transform your life?

Seeking honesty, or agreement?

Before we get too far, let's set the stage a bit so we don't let bias get the better of us. We say we want the truth and honesty from people, but when it comes right down to it, most of the time it's actually agreement we're looking for and hope to find. Let me save you the shock of discovering that you might *think* you want me to be honest & straight with you – but deep down, *you'll be listening for what you can believe and agree with*. Don't worry – that's normal.
Still, I'd like to offer you the opportunity to go from your normal way of being - to where you will receive the most benefit. How?
By *not* comparing what you know against what I'm sharing to see how it stands against your version of truth before you'll consider believing it. Being open to the possibility that there may be things you are not aware of that, when added to what you know and believe, may alter what you hold to be true.

Remember, **everything** you know and believe
 was at one time completely unknown to you -
  and you never even knew you didn't know it.

Savor that...

It's one of the reasons there isn't a Table of Contents in this book. I want every word, phrase, and paragraph to be untainted, unbiased, and void of any preconceived notions you may have about what you're about to read. EVERY part matters. If your goal is to merely skip ahead and skim through the book looking for what you want or think you'll find – I'd like to ask; How is that working out for you in the rest of your life?
A good deal of the content here relies on the knowing of several things – things that you may skip over in your rush to figure out what this book is about and how it compares to what you know. Stop your auto-pilot. Let go of your need to be right.
Don't do what you normally would do because that's all based on what you know and from YOUR past knowledge and experiences.

I don't want you to use what you *DO* know as an excuse
that prevents you from knowing what there **IS** to know.

Back to my earlier comment about my original intent.
The reason you're not getting some short-cut version of this is because I didn't want you to be short-changed.
Why? Simple. The best version of you impacts and affects those around you in a positive way, which tends to improve their lives as a result. This essentially causes a ripple effect across the pond of humanity, with each person's life made better in some way – and that "better" being passed forward... and forward... and forward. So, unless YOU choose to short-change yourself along the way and settle for chump change instead of stepping up and creating the life you want... you likely will have played a part in making the world a better place in the long run, which makes my life a better place. I thank you in advance!
We - you and I - have a vested interest in your success.
Keep that in mind throughout these pages, especially if I say something that may rub you the wrong way. I'm going to say things that need to be said because it benefits you to know.

For that reason, I've tried to address the "Why?" and "How?" questions that came up for me, as the reader, standing in your shoes (or more than likely sitting in your chair).
I knew if I didn't answer either one of these questions adequately enough to where you could at least say "OK, I can see that...", you'd experience confusion and just plow ahead through the book looking for something familiar or things you could agree with.
Well, we all know that a confused mind says "NO", because it's the easiest response and protects what we know. It's also true that if we only look for the familiar and what we agree with - we'll never discover everything else that can be found.
Fun fact, and possibly an example of something you're familiar with but didn't realize.
Do you know why there is a hole in the pull-tab of a soda can?
It's there to hold your straw in place.
Most people don't know that, even if they've opened hundreds of pop cans over the last 20 years.

Did you also know that when you FEEL good and when you FEEL healthy - you're going to have a clearer mind and make healthier decisions and better choices for your life?

Not only are there things you do not know,
there are those things you know something about
 - but may not know everything about them.
In both areas are a goldmine of opportunity.

I don't know everything.
You don't know everything.
We all know some things.
We're here to add to what we do know
and put it all to use in a very powerful way.
STOP!!!!
Don't skip this very important message.

As you read this book, you'll find points
that sound familiar and that you agree with.
Be mindful that *what you're reading* **is what is written**
 - not simply you thinking you know what I'm saying.
Don't skip parts because "you've heard this before".
Don't cheat yourself. You're worth more than that.
Also, if I say "You", and it doesn't pertain to you - insert the
word "They" or "Them". I tend to use the word "You" because
I'm speaking to *you* - not "Them", and since "They" are not here
with "Us", "We" are stuck discussing matters that affect all of
humanity as a whole.
So, in a way, you and I are presenting and representing
the Human Being in all manner of personal pronoun,
and I just don't want to have anyone miss out on
anything because of some grammatical grievance.

Now, being a human like myself, there may be times between
now and the final page of this book that a small voice in your
head might say something like;

"That's not right
I don't agree with this
That's not true
I don't agree with that
I don't think so
This isn't true
I disagree
That can't be right
No way
No no no
That's total BS!
I don't do that"

Perfect! That's how most excuses begin.

No need to be alarmed, it just means your subconscious is doing its job. From here forward, just to be clear, when I say "subconscious" I'm referring to the part of the mind/brain that we are not aware of nor have direct conscious control over.
What we know, the thoughts we have, and what we're aware of (conscious) is a minute fraction of what we actually know and are thinking about (subconscious).
Your subconscious mind's top priority is to keep you out of harm and within the comfort zone you currently reside in, so anything that attempts to push, pull, or otherwise compromise your being in that place of familiarity is going to be seen as a threat.
What you'll want to consider is that it doesn't matter WHERE you're being pulled - either to a better place or a worse place - THAT *you're being pulled* **out** *of it* is what is seen as the threat.

Got it?
Good!

I'm excited out of my gourd to be sharing this with you.
You see, I'm writing THIS part here after I finished the last page because I couldn't stand not sharing how amazing this is going to be for you. What's even better is that YOU are going to be as psyched if not more by the time you get to the end of the book!

* Critical thought to keep in mind throughout our time together.
Your mind & body is going to work for you - or against you.
The goal is to align both to work FOR you.

So, with this in mind - literally - I'm going to skip over the pleasantries and introductions and get right into it.
Your time is a most precious commodity,
and I don't want you to waste it.
Besides - I don't want you to use "I didn't have time
to read the book" as an excuse not to read it.

One more thing.
I left you room to take notes.
There are literally pages dedicated to your note taking.
It's as if I wanted to squash the excuse of "I wanted to take notes but didn't have any paper". I'm only meeting you halfway, though. Go get your own pen. Or pencil.

(*What a great time to practice Action over Excuse*)

As a connoisseur of excuses, with an impressive record of both creating and implementing them, I decided to conduct a study. My research crossed a broad spectrum of age, genre, race, sex, profession, nationality, color, creed, religion, background, and even across time itself (historical references).

After countless hours and pouring over endless data, a pattern began to emerge. A common thread and denominator had been found in virtually every case, and at last, with irrefutable proof in hand, I am able to submit my findings.

The conclusive evidence shows that, when it comes to excuses, **as long as the excuses are being used by the subject - they work.**

Every. Single. Time.

Regardless of the circumstance, situation, or scenario - when an excuse was used, it was effective.

What may surprise you the most is that the success of an excuse wasn't due to anyone's ability or inability.
It wasn't skill or talent - or the lack thereof.
It wasn't due to privilege or oppression.
There was actually no tangible aspect that determined the success of the excuse other than the person had to use it in order for it to work. With this in mind, we discover that it really isn't the excuse itself that matters - BUT THE APPLICATION of the excuse that gives it power.

Simply stated,
as long as you use an excuse, it will work -
regardless of what it is.

This could be good news, because it lets you off the hook from doing or achieving whatever it is that the excuse is excusing you from. For example, if you want to start your own business, but don't have enough capital, you can just use that (I didn't have the capital to get the business started) as the excuse.
This way you don't have to go through all the potential stress, probable setbacks, and possible failure that could occur for you. You can settle back into your comfort zone, become complacent with your accepted level of mediocrity, and talk to your friends and family about how you almost started your own business.

The excuse was used, and it worked - case closed, regardless of the fact that countless numbers of successful entrepreneurs began their business lacking the "necessary" funding.
They just didn't use it as an excuse and succeeded anyway.

Now here's where we turn a corner and I hope further consider the depth and impact that excuses have on us.

Again, what we know is that,
as long as you use an excuse,
it will work time and time again.
But the bitter truth of it is
you don't use excuses -
      your *excuses use you*,
- and use you up.
Day after day, excuse after excuse, they use you -
until finally, you have no more days left, leaving
your dreams flushed down a drain of pain and regret.

Realizing this is why you and I are here, with the goal of transforming the way we think and our way of being so that excuses no longer dictate our decisions or course of action.

The adverse conditions and conditioning of your life to this point has been comprised of many things, and the habit of living set in place to create your normal life is just that, a habit.
Just as there have been many factors and factions that have made You so, there are many tools that can help build what you want and Who - and each one put into play will get you there that much quicker.

Now, grab a pen or pencil - you'll want it soon.
If you don't do this, listen to the "Why" you don't
...and then go get a pen or pencil anyway.
You'll be glad you did.

Speaking of, though I penned this years ago,
it is especially relevant now.

"The biggest key to growing and going
beyond where you are is to realize
that you only know what you know.
Everything...
EVERYTHING that we know
we didn't know until we did.

It is one of the simplest yet profound truths.
Still, so many will overlook it and choose to
view the things around them through
the mirror of their past rather than
the looking glass of the present.

One of the biggest hurdles you will face in this World
is believing there is only one way to do something,
and you know what that is - and it is the best way.
Be open to the revelation that what you believe to be true
is based upon a minute portion of what is actually possible.
It could change many areas of your Life..."

Notes to self:

Think of something I already knew before I knew it.

_____
_____
_____
_____
_____
_____
_____
_____

* The landscape of what is unknown to you and that
you are completely unaware of is immeasurable, as are
the opportunities and possibilities that exist within it.

Origins of the excuse...

We know that the effectiveness of an excuse
isn't determined by a person's abilities or inabilities,
skill or talent, perceived privilege or oppression.

But where did the excuse come from to begin with?
Good question, and as you might suspect, from numerous places. What I'd like to begin with first are a few more conscious areas of thought more readily within our control. Because it's so common in today's world, let's look at how a certain "fairness factor" influences how readily you are able to develop an excuse. Generally speaking, "It's not fair" is, in itself, not an excuse, though it can at times have the same stopping power as any other excuse you use.
"It's not fair" gives a certain credibility to your excuse, especially if you believe it. Try it. Recall some excuse you've used for why you didn't do something.
I'm sure you've already done it, but add a "It's not fair" into your description and depiction of it. Notice how the excuse doesn't have to stand by itself any more where it can be picked apart, because when you add the "It's not fair" card into the equation, it divides the attention between the actual excuse and the "unfairness" of it. We can gain and gather support both from within ourselves as well as others as to how unfair our situation and scenario is - as if it were a real and true thing.

Let's unravel this.

Is Life fair?
Life is life.   There is no "fair" about it.
To each we are given one thing that matters: a LIFE.
We take our first breath, and beyond that, what we do with what we have, give, and receive will determine where we will go and how far. When you start caving in to the blame game that "fair" is, you will only carve the rut of your life deeper and deeper - and to the heights you are capable of you cannot soar when mired in the mud of blame, complaint, and what is "fair" and "unfair". Opportunities and obstacles surround us ALL in more abundance than we can ever take advantage of - and can take us further than we can ever imagine, or stop us in every undertaking we pursue.
Yes, I said opportunities AND obstacles.
Oftentimes, they can be the same thing!

Life offers it all up to us, and it is up to us how we will put each to use. YOU decide for yourself if you are going to use "fair" to influence what you do and don't do in and for your Life.

Now, the concept of "fair" is heavily comprised of comparison, and because comparison is so prevalent in the way we live - let's twist it to our advantage in a way that serves us.

Question for you:

Who do you need to see
do the thing you want to do
before you will finally say
"All right, if THEY can do it, I CAN DO IT!"

Because up until now, typically when you see people who are successful, there is always a reason for it that is not within your own grasp and that you believe is beyond your reach.

You think things like:
They were born with it.
They came from a wealthy family.
They were smart.
They were just lucky.
They knew the right people.
They took advantage of people.
They had a good education.
They brown-nosed.
Their timing was right.
They were gifted.
They were naturally talented.

Unlike you:
They weren't raised in an abusive home.
They didn't have asthma, ADD, ADHD, dyslexia, diabetes, allergies, or some other health challenge.
They weren't born with the "wrong" color of skin, or of a foreign nationality, or from a "bad" neighborhood.
They weren't shy, talk with a stutter, or suffer from anxiety, depression, or other labeled illness.
They weren't dumb, teased, ridiculed, or bullied.
They weren't unwanted or unloved.
And the list goes on.

Somehow, successful people had
(*insert something you didn't have* **HERE**)
and DIDN'T have to deal with
(*insert what you think kept you from being successful* **HERE**),
and *THAT*'s why they succeeded - and why you can't.

There is always some reason why they can, and you can't - and you'll go to the ends of the earth to "prove" both.

I'll also bet that I can find people who are successful despite any of those same reasons and beyond. Trust me - I've done my homework. Not long ago I even found out about a baby boy who had been abandoned in a dumpster, and by the time he was in his mid-20s had become a self-made millionaire. Talk about tough beginnings! And for those who are comfortable using race as one of their go-to excuses, he is black.

It just goes to show that it's not where you start that matters; it's when you decide to get going - and get off your excuses - that makes the difference.
So many people spend their time complaining about where they are, where they came from - as if it should somehow earn them credit toward success simply because they "put in their time". It doesn't. And I hate to break it to you, but even though the starting line begins at the same point for everyone (*Where* you start) - the race is easier for some than it is for others.
There are countless people who will have to work a LOT harder than you will, and you know what? Some won't. Yes, some will actually have fewer obstacles than you. Some won't have to work as hard. Some won't be carrying as much baggage (because they discovered they could go faster by leaving it behind). (Read that again)
Take note:
We all have a past. Every one of us.
And something about it – our past - is often our biggest excuse. It's always there, ready to give us a hand and pull us back to its familiarity and comfort zone that is rationally so uncomfortable.

You can let your past rule you with its fears and "failures" reminding you of your every perceived weakness and inability, or you can allow it to be a source to draw wisdom from and learn the lessons it has to teach. If you haven't realized it yet, being a constant visitor of and living in your past will have you cowering from anything that reminds you of your negative experiences.

And, since you are always on the lookout to avoid things that resemble the negatives of the past, you will shape both opportunity and unknown into those familiar fears and failures.
You will in every way create what you don't want for your future because you keep carrying it forward from your past.
People don't move forward with their lives by always looking backward. Try walking forward while looking behind you. You'll trip, fall, and most likely end up getting hurt, right?

It's easy to point to the past and say "That is why I can't" - and use it as an excuse for the present today.
But let me repeat - you really aren't using an excuse.
The excuse is using you - and using up your life.

Now, I touched on this earlier, but this might be a good time to let you know that my usual dosage of sugar coating may not always be present throughout our time here. I ask that you take nothing personally - only that you take it to heart and heed the message, knowing it to be beneficial.

Our level of being coddled in society has left us anemic to the courage that previous generations have enjoyed. Common sense is often overruled by comfort level, and political correctness has us splitting hairs and mincing words to appease people who will always blame everyone but themselves for where they are and for what is happening in every area of their life.
IF I say things at times that may seem cold and callous - it is not because I don't care, but because I care enough to be real with you and let you know that resolution to the issues and challenges in your life are your responsibility to undertake; just as mine are for me to resolve.

Here's something that you may or may not be aware of.
Regardless of your IQ, you're smart enough to come up with one excuse after another that would convince most of us (first and foremost yourself) as to why you "can't" do something, be something, or achieve any number of things you'd like.
You're actually borderline brilliant at times, truth be told.
I'll be unraveling and revealing more about this later on, but for now let's just say you may not be aware (consciously) of just how creative and capable you really are at making excuses.

To put it short & sweet -
your subconscious knows more than your "woke" self ever will about making excuses - it's been doing it your whole life!

And guess what?
Whoever you are, I guarantee that I can find someone with fewer abilities, less talent, bigger obstacles, and far more excuses than you and I put together, who managed to turn whatever your "can't" is into a "DONE. NEXT!".

Try me.
No, seriously - please!
I'd love for you to parade all your reasons for why you gave up instead of stepping up and settled for quitting.
Harsh? For some, maybe.
Why? The truth hurts, and I've had my own fair share of excuses rule over me in the past - just like you do!
Like me, I hope you're tired of hearing the same old excuses year after year as to why you don't do this, why you don't do that, why you're not this or that.
I really hope you're sick and tired of hearing new & creative excuses spewing out of your mouth as to why you're not where you want to be or doing what you want to do.
Excuses are using you - and using up your life.

Forget whatever noise in your head that might say otherwise - I happen to know that you are many times more awesome and able to not only do what you think you **can** but all the more *what you think you can't*, so forgive me if I'm slightly ticked that you've settled for so much less from yourself!
You should be mad at yourself for taking pennies on the dollar for what you're worth and accepting such a pittance from Life.
Seriously, if you can't get inspired or motivated enough to make changes in your life, I hope you can at least get mad enough to. It's not a place to make lasting change from, but it can at least get you walking toward it!

After all, aren't you sick and tired of settling for trinkets when such an abundance of treasure abounds?

I thought this next "exercise" might give us a chance to catch our breath and calm down a bit.
Yes, "us". We're in this together!
Incidentally, there are times when it may seem like the topic of excuses isn't the only thing being covered in this book.
It's not your imagination.
Let's put it this way.
If you're in a boat that's taking on water - I don't want to leave you with only a really great mop to clean up the mess.
I want to help you fix the leak!
There are reasons Why you knowingly and not so knowingly make excuses.
Wouldn't it be great to break the cycle of excuses that throw us off track in the first place?
What if you didn't have to deal with the circus of excuses that keeps you from what you want every day?

Remember when I asked you to grab a pen or pencil?
Great if you did, and if you still don't have one, you now have a great example of excuses working if you use them.
You also have another opportunity to break the cycle and rise above your excuse and play with the rest of us who are prepared.

Here is a question I hope you learn to ask of yourself often.
Are you participating
fully in the Present
or simply performing
replays of the Past?

Take some time to go through these two charts, both Past and Present, starting with Past, and be very real with your answers:

Past goals:		Obstacles:

Past dreams:		Obstacles:

Past desires:		Obstacles:

Past wants:		Obstacles:

Past passions:		Obstacles:

Past hopes:		Obstacles:

For those above that are no longer on your Present list below - jot down what finally had you decide not to pursue them. Don't be casual about this. If you don't know why, you'll likely be able to use that excuse again and again. Be clear.

_____
_____
_____
_____
_____
_____
_____
_____
_____
_____
_____
_____
_____
_____
_____
_____
_____
_____
_____
_____
_____
_____
_____
_____
_____
_____
_____
_____
_____
_____
_____
_____

Now, let's look at Present:

Present goals: || Obstacles:
_____||_____
_____||_____
_____||_____
_____||_____
_____||_____

Present dreams: || Obstacles:
_____||_____
_____||_____
_____||_____
_____||_____
_____||_____

Present desires: || Obstacles:
_____||_____
_____||_____
_____||_____
_____||_____
_____||_____

Present wants: || Obstacles:
_____||_____
_____||_____
_____||_____
_____||_____
_____||_____

Present passions: || Obstacles:
_____||_____
_____||_____
_____||_____
_____||_____
_____||_____

Present hopes: || Obstacles:
_____||_____
_____||_____
_____||_____
_____||_____
_____||_____

What is different about your Present List vs your Past List and what difference is there determining your success?

Looking back on your list of (PAST) Obstacles -
do any of them look more like excuses now in the present?

You see, I'm not the same person I was last month.
Neither are you.
We've seen, heard, and learned new things since then.
More than we know!
We have gained insight and awareness
as well as experience and perspective.

Keep in mind, all of this happens far more on a subconscious level than a conscious level. Even if you can't think of any way in which you think or believe differently than you did a week, month, or year ago - the elements are within you that could and would alter the outcome of your endeavors.
(Later I'll cover just how much - it's incredible to grasp)
You may even come to realize that an excuse you used in the past could now become a driving force in your success!
A book that held no real value a month ago, today could lead to a breakthrough in an area that you've been stuck for years.
Techniques and strategies, once tried in a previously biased and prejudiced mindset, may not have produced positive results - but may now actually change your life when you add who you are now and what you know TODAY to them.

Understand the power of being in the present -
of not reliving and repeating the familiarity of the past.
Grasp how much of what you do and believe in your day to day life is a replay of yesterdays gone by – a programming of how you'll live, what you'll do, see, and be based on what you've done, seen, and been in the past.

Every day holds opportunities and obstacles, and your ability to discern and determine one from the other grows daily - allowing you to learn from the known and unknown alike.

Keep in mind that your day to day life is based on a pattern of familiarity, and the past is coloring your future by painting over the present. The end result is that you won't really "see" what's right there in front of you *or all around you* if it doesn't resemble what you know.

No matter what our pursuit in Life, we tend to look
for its discovery within the confines of the known.

This might seem like a good place to start, yet it's also where we typically get stuck, because what we know is so limited.

If you can hold a place for your self where you remain open to allowing the unknown to play a part in your success - you will experience countless opportunities. The unknown will become your friend and ally, rather than an enemy that you fear, and the realm of possibility will be your playground.

Currently you are going through Life with a certain degree of bias or "listening" in your journey to discovery for what is important, and what is not - what is relevant, and what is not, and what is helpful, and what is not.
The challenge is, you are severely narrowing the realm of possibilities and opportunities that exist for you to within only what *you believe and know as such* to be discovered.
That which *you* do not deem important,
relevant, or helpful - you ignore.
What this means in application is that most of the best ideas and solutions to getting what you want *are getting away from you.* When you can't make your perceived solutions work, **you make excuses** to justify, blame, defend, and explain your "couldn't".

This revelation alone is going to escalate your awareness and allow you to discover opportunities hidden in plain sight.

The thing I want to look at now is...

the **Want**.

Nothing will work unless YOU WANT IT TO
- and unless YOU want what you want, your attempts
to achieve & receive it will be unsuccessfully met,
with excuse after excuse as to why.

These things that you say you Want -
goals, dreams, desires, wants, passions, hopes;
this place you want to be, the kind of life you want to lead...
Do you REALLY want that, or is it a story
that you've made up that sounds good?
Is this "Want" motivated out of pressure,
or perhaps a "Should" planted by others?
*Note to Self –
"Keeping up with the Joneses" rarely transforms your life.

You'll always come up with excuses -
and excuses will always come up for you
 - if **YOU** really don't Want what you say you want.

You may tell others that you want to live in a mansion
overlooking the ocean, but truthfully the idea of a cabin in the
woods on the edge of a stream is Heaven to you.
Guess what?
You're going to sabotage your ability to afford a mansion,
and the collateral will keep you from getting either one!

Do you really want to find inner happiness?
Do you want more abundance in your life?
Do you want a healthy, vibrant body?
Do you want a better relationship with yourself and others?

These sound like no-brainers.
I mean, who wouldn't right??

But if you really found a way to have it all and more... wouldn't that scare you?

It might. Because changing any relationship with yourself will create feelings and reactions that are not only very scary - they will remove you far from your comfort zone.   It is far more comfortable to aspire and complain than it is to actually do anything that will help create the life you say you want. You know where you are and somehow it feels safe to you, even if you know you could have more - even if you are dying to have something different in your life.

Think about it. Is this true for you?
Notice that your excuses are really your fear talking.

People say they want more happiness, more money, better health, closer relationships, a more satisfying love life, and a whole list of things that aren't going quite the way they'd like them to.
So they *say*.
Yet, whatever state these areas of life are in now is their accepted "standard", and it's often expected.
It's what they know. They've accepted it as how things are. And however uncomfortable it is; it's the comfort level they've been conditioned to call "normal".
What we settle for becomes the standard for our life, and we don't see or accept solutions and opportunities that would break us out of our status quo.

What's that you say?

"You don't know me. You don't know my life."
"You don't know how I live day to day - what I need to deal with every day."
"You don't know my struggles and my pain, and everything I've got going against me."

I get it. I'm not trying to lecture you from some pulpit or stage - I'm out here on the field with you.
I know some of the thoughts you have - I've had them, too!

I don't need to know the details of your life, or all your problems in specific. But you tell me - do you find yourself living in a state of being that often says, "That's just the way it is"?

It's a common mindset, when your solutions in the moment don't solve the problems at hand, to feel and think that way.
You can make various statements about any area of your life that indicate you've tried everything, and nothing works.
Time after time I hear people say (when various strategies, solutions, and techniques are offered) things like;
"Oh, I tried that. It doesn't work"
"That didn't work for me"
"That doesn't work for me"
"My friend did that. It didn't help her"
"So and so tried that & it never worked"

AS IF these were actual reasons to stop trying!
Don't be fooled - they are excuses.
You've probably heard before that Thomas Edison failed 1000 times before he invented the light bulb. Toss that aside.
Here's one of the answers he gave someone who asked how he felt about "failing" so many times.
"I didn't fail 1,000 times. The light bulb
 was an invention with 1,000 steps."
Truth be told, he didn't even "invent" the light bulb. Versions of the electric light bulb had been in existence since the early 1800s. Edison didn't begin his own serious research until 1878. What Edison did, in a nutshell, was to create a more viable light bulb; one that could be made available to the masses, had a higher level of longevity, and was cost effective for its use. He quite literally made the lightbulb a household name and fixture in many ways.

I'm getting off track.
My point is that he didn't fail at any point.
What he did was test nearly numerous components (some say well over 4,000) that ended up not meeting his criteria.
In his own words;
 "I was never myself discouraged,
 or inclined to be hopeless of success."
With every try and trial, there was something to learn, and the knowledge that was available as a result grew exponentially.
And (regarding the filament, which was the major piece of his experiments) he didn't merely try one thing, then another - he also combined materials in hopes that aspects of both working together would achieve the end result desired.

I don't think at any point did Edison say or believe
"Well, THAT didn't work, so I'm sure THIS won't".

He didn't use a result (labeled by many as "failure")
as an excuse to give up on the goal, nor allow it
to detract or determine his next steps.
Here's a fun fact. Traditional light bulbs have used a tungsten filament for nearly 100 years. Yet initially, this wasn't Edison's doing. It was among his list of possibilities, but at the time he first experimented with his own light bulb creation he lacked the technology that would make it a viable choice. In other words, he couldn't make it work to satisfy his end goal.
Do you know what he did end up using?
Bamboo. Now, just between you me, and the fencepost - would you ever have thought of bamboo to use with electricity?!
He did combine it with another substance, for the record.
Good tip there, btw

Now, we'd all like to have a guaranteed game plan for achieving what we want in life - one that is penciled out and described in great detail. But, unless you're 3 years old, by now you know that it may take some trial and error.
It may also include things we might never have considered, wouldn't believe possible, and don't think would work!
There are solutions and avenues to achieve what you want in life that aren't even on your radar.
As a matter of fact, that is exactly where most of them are; in the realm of the unknown... TO YOU.
Yet rather than take the next step that would get you closer to it - you pull an excuse card out of your deck and play it.

JUST BECAUSE YOU
don't know every step of the path,
does that mean you stop walking?

"But what if I'm walking toward a cliff?"
"But what if there are landmines?"
"But what if there is quicksand?"
"But what if I get attacked?"
"But what if I get lost?"

Don't be a **"But"** head.
Stop filling your mind with negative "Buts" and "What if" fears.

Here's the only kind of "But what if" thoughts I suggest you hang on to:

"BUT WHAT IF I SUCCEED?"
"BUT WHAT IF IT WORKS?"
"BUT WHAT IF I MAKE IT?"

When Edison used beard hair - yes, BEARD HAIR - as a possible filament choice for the light bulb, regardless of whether it worked or not, it took him a step closer to what DID work.
Can you imagine him sitting there, brainstorming ideas for a filament just as two of his employees, sporting very full beards, walk by, and all of a sudden he thinks; "Hmmmm... beard hair?" followed by a chuckle of disbelief, and then - "BUT WHAT IF IT WORKS?". Imagine how crazy they must've thought HE was when he called them over and plucked a hair from each of their beards. What went through their minds as they watched him attach the hair between the contact wires and seal the test bulb? What did they think when he threw the power switch, and saw... Nothing. No light. No smoke. Nothing.
Another failure, right?

Au contraire!

An outcome occurred. **That's what happened**.
Actions were taken that produced a result,
and that result became part of the journey
on the path to discovery and eventual success.
He didn't use an unwanted result (labeled by many as "failure") as an excuse to give up on the mission, nor allow it to detract or determine his next steps.

The experiences of your life and the things that happen are just that; things that happen and experiences. Similarly, the actions you take in life produce *outcomes* - not failure, not success.
From each take what there is to gain from the experience.

This is where so many get tripped up.
We tend to get caught up in believing that we know what progress looks like and the path it should take.
Preconceived notions about what should happen or could happen often skew our view of everything that actually *does* happen.
By focusing on and looking for the evidence that supports our beliefs, we often limit our ability to see what is possible to within the confines of that bias.

So, before you come to a conclusion about something you did that "failed" or "didn't work out", ask yourself this.

What do I believe about what happened that might be preventing me from seeing all that actually happened? Are the results based on an observation of reality or a biased reflection of my own expectations and past experiences? Have I put anything into the space that would skew my ability to be open to all possibilities? What meaning have I given to what happened?

We aren't as apt to make excuses once we realize that what is possible or impossible is determined far more by our approach and execution, coupled with the meaning we give to what happened.

If we choose to view unfavorable results only as failure or something to fear, both our conscious and subconscious will go into self-defense mode - preventing us from putting ourselves into situations that resemble failure or threat to our security. This would include, but is not limited to, anything that might make us feel bad, look bad to others, feel insecure, be rejected, feel unloved, look stupid, be disrespected, be unaccepted, feel unworthy; basically anything that makes us feel "less than" and threatens our comfort zone or current level of health.

The easiest, and often automatic way to do this, is by using an excuse; an excuse as to why we failed, why we shouldn't try again, and why we're right about it.

IF YOU teach and train yourself to understand that the experiences of your life and the things that happen are just that; **things that happen and experiences**, then you will be able to recognize and shut down your excuse response and move forward in every area of your life!

Exercise in Awareness

Here is an exercise to sharpen your level of awareness. This is worthy of your time, so I hope you'll participate.

I want you to question what you do. I want you to take yourself off of autopilot from the time you wake up to the time you go to bed. If you're really serious about being serious - start a journal of this and keep track.

Every day, pay attention to what you do and
   ask yourself **why** you're doing it,
   and **how** is it benefiting you?

When your alarm clock rings (and I'm going to suggest setting it 15 minutes earlier than usual) ask yourself why you're waking up at this time, and how is it benefiting you?
Of course, there are some things that might seem a bit ridiculous, like taking a shower, for example.
"Why am I doing this? How is it benefiting me?"
But you know what? Asking these two questions, even though it sounds simple, can open up an amazing dialogue for other areas - that's why I suggest a journal and to not overlook an area of your life, no matter how minute or mundane it may seem.
Putting on deodorant, cologne, perfume, makeup?
Ask yourself "Why am I doing this? How is it benefiting me?"
The things you eat or don't eat for breakfast;
"Why am I doing this? How is it benefiting me?"
The clothes you wear;
"Why am I doing this? How is it benefiting me?"
Lighting a cigarette;
"Why am I doing this? How is it benefiting me?"
Driving to work;
"Why am I doing this? How is it benefiting me?"
The decisions you make in your work;
"Why am I doing this? How is it benefiting me?"
What you have for lunch, snack;
"Why am I doing this? How is it benefiting me?"
Going to the movies;
"Why am I doing this? How is it benefiting me?"
Going to a nightclub or a bar for drinks;
"Why am I doing this? How is it benefiting me?"
Meeting up with someone;
"Why am I doing this? How is it benefiting me?"
You get the drift.

Ready for the fun part?
Try to see your reasons & justifications
for what you do in all of these things.

Again, we are used to running our lives on autopilot – so
paying attention to these things is not going to be "normal".
But you know what?
I've never seen "normal" pay off in a great way.

I've never seen a "normal" way of living
create an extraordinary life – only mediocre.
I've never known anyone to transform their life following
the "normal" paths and common routines of the day.
I've never known "normal" to make a meaningful
or positive change in this world, sorry to say.

I *have* seen "normal" convince people to believe that
"It is what it is" and that the power to change their present
situation is out of their hands and beyond their control.
I have seen "normal" cause people to spend the best hours
and the best days of their life devoted to paying bills and
planning vacations to get away from where they're
spending the best hours and best days of their life.
I've seen "normal" clog the highways with people
going where they didn't want to go, and others
coming from places they didn't want to be.
I've known "normal" to sell every soul short who would accept it
and strip possibility and potential from anyone who embraced it.

Those who create an uncommon life are willing to put in more
than what is commonly expected of average, "normal" people.
Each of us is capable of the extraordinary,
yet most of us act out our lives in ordinary ways.
We want more, yet are often unwilling to do more;
hoping and praying for better - never acting on faith that it will.

We trade our precious time for the mere reflection of treasure,
and lower our expectation of life to what others award us.
Yet the "average" who are content to merely sip from
the wells of abundance have no more nor fewer hours
in a day than those who drink deeply of it.

What I have observed is that people who create extraordinary
lives do not waste their time complaining about circumstances;
they are too busy creating and causing their own to occur.

They sacrifice short term amusements
for the long term and meaningful.
They are more purpose driven rather than pleasure seeking.
They don't blame the past or point fingers at people.
They find reasons to persevere - not excuses to quit.

Extraordinary people understand this:

The circumstances of our lives do not determine our situation.
We do. We choose.

What I can tell you is that if you find yourself complaining about
your life - it's a condition of your heart, your lack of hope.
It isn't your perceived failures that reveal your "limits" in
this life - it is where you've placed and misplaced your faith.
You've convinced yourself that Life isn't fair, and you're right.
You believe that nothing goes your way, and it doesn't.
You wait for the next bad thing to happen, and soon it does.
You tell yourself that no matter what you do,
or how hard you try, nothing turns out –
And you're proven right again and again.
You do not see the solutions to your problems
because your belief keeps you blind to them.
No matter how many opportunities surround you,
no matter how inundated with possibilities you are -
your belief and faith that none exist make it so!

Stop and think how powerful that is.
You, with your belief and faith alone,
cause and create the very life you expect.
Most people have a misconception that faith and
belief is a positive force that will bring about good.
I'd like you to consider that it is more like a wind;
where you direct it - is where it will take you.

Again - do you see how amazing this is?
Can you even catch a glimpse of how powerful you are?

May I be blunt here?
If your life sucks, you should be getting excited by now.
Do you know how truly powerful you must be to ward off
the spoils and opportunities that surround you every day?!?
Imagine if you sought to steer in a more positive direction.

Once you truly believe Life is more than fair,
you'll be blessed beyond compare. Once you **act**
as if things will go your way, it's a done deal.
Expect good things to happen, and others will be
amazed at how so many good things happen to you.

Do you even know how great your Life could be??

The answer is where you start.

And maybe I'm being selfish here, but
I want you to have an exceptional life
so that not only are *you* able to soar,
but that you might also uplift others
that they can learn to fly as well...

I'm going to expound more on this next statement later,
yet for now understand that merely because there
may not be an obvious or direct connection *for you*
between excuses and various things I've shared
doesn't mean they aren't there and don't exist.
What there is to consider is that, relatively speaking,
we are trying to grasp orchestrations of the infinite
within the comprehension of the finite.

Defining moments

You are the one defining what your experiences mean.
You are the one giving meaning to the things that happen.
When you attach negative meanings to things, your mind is going to "excuse" you from it happening again and shelter you from being put in those positions. You will believe you're being protected from the unknown, unfamiliar, and feared; yet what you really are is being trapped in your comfort zone of familiarity and in a place you feel you belong and are worthy of being.

The challenge with this is that the majority of solutions for what has you feel stuck, and that you can't seem to break out of, exist outside of your comfort zone - beyond the familiar and what you know. The majority of opportunities available in your life surround you every day yet remain out of sight.
Why is this?

Because your deepest levels of belief
will create the outcome for both
positive and negative results
and allow you to see and reveal
the evidence that would support it,
and obscure and hide what doesn't.

If in your core you don't believe good will come your way, your mind will very creatively uncover the results you expect.
Let's take a moment to reframe this a bit.
For those familiar with computers, most of them have a "Search" feature where you can enter a keyword and the computer will search for files containing that word. In addition, it will not bring up files that do NOT contain that word, essentially filtering out everything that does not contain that word.

Consider that you move through the world with a mind that is filtering out everything except for what you've entered as "keywords". The keywords of your life are the truths and beliefs that you hold, and your subconscious locates those things that contain supporting data and conceals that which doesn't contain your "truth".

There is a phrase that I think we all know;
"Seeing is believing".
Yet through the ages it has been revealed in many ways
that *Believing* plays a significant role in our *Seeing*.
One could say that faith is one of the most familiar aspects of
this; that if we truly believe in something, we will see it come to
fruition. Adversely, until we believe in a thing to be seen, it will
not be revealed.

If you don't believe you deserve, are worthy of, or capable of
more than your present conditions and circumstances - your
subconscious will filter out opportunities and components that
might lead you to rise above where you are.
You will pass by the building blocks of your dreams because your
mind won't allow you to see them - or see them for what they
could be. You will remain blind to the potential within yourself
and your surroundings until you shift your level of belief and
expectation of self.

To your favor, the opposite holds true as well. If in your core
you believe good things happen, they often do.
Whatever label or causality you would like to
attach to this, the end result is still the same.
You affect your life far more than you know,
and only a fraction of the time are you aware of it.

So, let's dig a bit into the science of why we so often can't see
what would benefit us, as well as why we too often find
ourselves face to face with the things that are detrimental.
The first step of this awareness is
to be aware of how unaware we are!
Arguably 99% of your excuses, your reasons, your thoughts,
decisions, and actions all originate from a place that is out of
sight, out of mind. For good reason, of course.

Have you ever tried taking a sip of water from a fire hydrant?
I don't suggest it - the sheer force alone could possibly knock
you unconscious, let alone that you'd drown in no time at all.

That being said, the waters of Life are coming at you at 400
gallons a second, and if you try to take it all in - you'll drown!
There are many studies and numerous reports that vary in
statistics, yet for the average person in the U.S. it is estimated
that each day our senses receive (in kb of data) the equivalent
of 16,393 copies of Gone With The Wind.

Keep in mind, "Gone With The Wind" is over 1000 pages long!
Did I also mention **each day** this occurs?

According to the Encyclopedia Britannica, our brain is receiving 11 million bits per second - yet the conscious mind is only able to process 50 bits per second. That's a conservative estimate, for the record. If you do your homework, you'll find that this number (11,000,000) is considerably lower than what newer studies would indicate. What everyone will agree on, though, is that it's virtually impossible to determine the incredible amount of input we're exposed to, and that the subconscious processes well over 220,000 times what our conscious is able to - some even say a million times more.
That's .000045%
For a bit of visual perspective, picture an Olympic sized swimming pool. *It holds over 660,000 gallons* of water.
That's 18,000 bathtubs.
Now, take **1** quart out.
That, in perspective, is what you know.
A bit humbling, eh?
That's what you were able to be aware of,
make sense of, interpret, and understand.
Correction. That's what you were ALLOWED to be aware of, make sense of, interpret, and understand.

In essence, you were saved from drowning in 660,000 gallons of water (information), and merely splashed with a quart.

1 Quart = **Conscious Mind**

x 18,000

= **Sub Conscious Mind**

now imagine this page
and 900 more pages just like it.

Let's take a look for a moment in real time – right now.
There are 3 clocks in the room next to me, each one ticking slightly out of synch of the other. The heater is on -
I can feel a slight breeze of warm air on my right arm.
I can hear the motor of the water distiller running in the kitchen.
Now I can hear the drops of water falling into the glass pitcher as they condense out of evaporation.
The heater just kicked off. I can hear the metal coils clicking as they cool. The hard drive of my computer is growling away as background programs run. The refrigerator just kicked on, and the lights dimmed for a brief second. My right foot has a slight ache when I tense it. I can feel a loose hair resting on my left shoulder. To my right is a massive disarray of books, CDs, DVDs, papers, and things that need organized "someday".
On my left is a fireplace, and near it an open bag of potting soil that should be somewhere else. There are 2 chairs next to the couch that never made it back into the dining room after guests were entertained, along with a pillow that belongs on a bed somewhere. In the corner is a piano with sheet music and books piled around it, and a small Christmas tree sitting on the end - hoping nobody would notice Christmas was 3 months ago.
It would take hours to discover and describe everything that is around and within me in these few moments of time.
And, as if that wasn't enough - I am both surrounded and saturated by varying forms of radiation.
Radioactive elements around me and even within my own body are emitting ionizing radiation as they decay.
Rays of infrared and ultraviolet, radio waves, microwaves, x-rays, gamma-rays, and even cosmic rays not of this world permeate my body without my conscious self being aware of it - yet able to affect me all the same.

I, like you, am inundated and overwhelmed by hundreds... thousands of things that are never really noticed, and only a fraction of it all are we consciously aware of UNTIL we begin taking the time to become aware of the everything that is there.

Not only is that incredibly profound, but it is an example of how our mind can fade and block out those things that aren't really relevant to know in the moment, or those things that it has determined are not beneficial to its (perceived) well-being.

Our conscious mind, for the most part, is on a "Need to know" basis. Everything I listed above as an observation would have gone unnoticed had I not intentionally stopped to observe all that I could sense around me.

My ears were hearing everything, whether I was aware of the sounds or not. My nose could smell the cinnamon pine cones leftover from Christmas near the heater when it kicked on, even if I hadn't "noticed". I saw the green tape around the bunch of bananas in the kitchen, even if I didn't "see" it as I sat here at the table writing this.

I was kept from being overwhelmed and drowned in sensory overload by my brain's filtering and defensive capabilities. Truly, I believe, that if we were made consciously aware of everything that existed within our realm of capacity to detect, it would send us into a catatonic state. We just couldn't handle it.

What has this got to do with making excuses? A LOT. Because you really have no idea why you make excuses, let alone how often you do - even when you think you do. You can't imagine the amount of off-the-radar thought and calculation that went into making the reasons you have done and haven't done virtually and literally everything in your life.

I don't want to bore you with the biological mechanics, but it might help to cover a few of the fundamentals and set a base. We all know what our primary senses are: Sight, Sound, Smell, Taste, Touch. These essentially let your inner world know what the outer world is up to, AND we are typically consciously aware to a minute degree of their input. The sun shining, a dog barking, hot apple pie baking, tart lemonade, a hug.

We tend to notice these kinds of interactions with our environment on a conscious level. Beyond this, thanks to certain parts of our brain and the systems tied to them, we DON'T notice the countless other things that are happening at the same time. We don't hear the 12th airplane flying overhead in the past hour, or the 3 clocks ticking nearby. We don't see the crows lined up on the power lines, nor take note that there were 165 trees in each row that we passed by over the last 1/4 mile of our road trip.

The examples are endless.

If you're interested in the *How* so much is filtered from our conscious awareness, I invite you to research the primary factions involved, beginning with the RAS (Reticular Activating System). Dig also into the roles of the Prefrontal cortex and Amygdala, the Thalamus and Hypothalamus, and how the Limbic system ties in. It's a good start, and you may be surprised at how much you take for granted is handled by your brain.
How our mind works with the body as a whole, as well as the individual parts working together to affect both our internal functions as well as external interaction in our world is mind bogglingly miraculous in its orchestration.

For the sake of valuing your time, though, we'll focus more on the impact they have rather than the How.

The good and the bad news of this filtering effect
is that these systems are calling the shots as to
what you "should" and "shouldn't" be aware of.
While ultimately designed to protect you,
they are also responsible for blinding and
blocking you from seeing many opportunities
among the abundance of possibilities that exist.

Here's a quick example of what I would call positive mind filtering. My favorite time is 12:34, and it happens twice every day. It's one of the many simple pleasures that occur in my life. If I had a nickel for every time I glanced at a clock and noticed that the time was 12:34 - I'd have a nice little nest egg! Some might say that those scenarios are a sign from the universe, or some other exterior causality or force. I may touch on this in more depth another time, but for now let us consider that you are a highly sophisticated composite of sensory, diagnostic, and computing capabilities many times beyond the greatest supercomputer ever built. If you think we do not possess the ability to determine the time of day based on both exterior data and our own internal "clock", then you vastly underestimate the human potential. Have you ever known people who can just wake up without an alarm clock - and it didn't matter what time they went to bed or what time they needed to wake up? Child's play for the brain.

There are 3 clocks within my range of sight right now, and a time / date indicator on my computer screen in the bottom right-hand corner. I haven't looked at any of them directly for a while now, but if the need to know what time it was became imperative, I would be made aware of the time. As I type this, I know that the sensors responsible for sight are already taking in the face of the clock in the living room as well as the clock in the bottom right hand corner of the computer I'm typing on. My subconscious "sees" what time it is; the information is there. So, when 12:34 rolls around and my subconscious decides I could use a bit of positive stimuli, it gives me a little nudge that prompts me to look at some time keeping device.
Well, now. Would you look at the time? 12:34!
If I had a nickel...

With every car I've ever owned, I began seeing others like it nearly everywhere I went after I bought them. Whether going down the road, parked on a side street, in the rear-view mirror, or in a parking lot - they practically jump out of the woodwork. Am I looking for them? No. Was I not seeing them before? No. (Some of you may have thought the right answer was "Yes") Prior to the purchase of my particular car, there was no reason for my conscious to be made aware of them specifically, so they faded into the background of "grey" that has no importance in the moment; out of sight, out of (conscious) mind... but not out of subconscious mind.
When there was an attachment made with the car, VIOLA!!! The subconscious colored the grey of the obscure and marked it to be noticed by the conscious. Speaking of color, cobalt blue jumps out at me wherever I go. It is my favorite color.

Another more important and useful example I'll share is when my son disappeared while we were at the fair when he was about 6 years old. It didn't matter that I couldn't remember what he was wearing or that I couldn't see him among the hundreds of people there. As I walked around, my subconscious DID know what he was wearing, even though I couldn't for the life of me recall. It knew the color of his hair both in the shade as well as in the sunlight, and even his spatial dimensions as compared to those around him. Needless to say, I found him rather quickly - safe and sound, in want of an elephant ear. Have I mentioned yet how beyond conceivable our subconscious is compared to our cognizant awareness?
Just checking.

I'll tell you what happened to me last weekend, because it ties in well with all of this. My glasses are somewhere in the Pacific Ocean. For those of you who are familiar with the story of "The Star Thrower" - that was me Sunday afternoon. Instead of starfish, though, it was clams I found on the beach. I picked up the ones washed ashore that I believed to be alive, walked out into the water, and flung them out to sea for a second chance. I suspect it was one of my life-saving throws that caused my glasses, normally hanging from my jacket, to fall into the shallows of the shore, where they were sucked out into the ebbing abyss of the Lincoln City coastline. It was almost sunset when I discovered the spectacles were gone, and my search for them was met only by the laughter of seagulls and waves.
I had an old set of specs in the glovebox, so they suited me well enough to get home. After 4 days of wearing them - they remind me of how much clearer things can be seen with the right prescription.
Now, things that were once seen clearly are now fuzzy. Details are hazy. It's difficult to recognize things for what they are, and easy to mistake things for what they aren't.

So, I've got to ask you -
How is your sight?
How clear is your vision??
Consider that the "prescription" of your beliefs and opinions tend to skew and slant the reality that IS against what you perceive and can see. As I'm walking around with my glasses on now, my mind is seeing only a partial view of what is, and my mind is filling in the blanks with what it believes is there based on what it knows - from a collection of data / knowledge built on past experiences and learned beliefs.
Yet, all of this is being seen and viewed, again, through the "correctional lenses" of beliefs and opinions.
You know that phrase "seeing is believing"?
Consider that what you believe… is what you are seeing. And what you don't believe - remains fuzzy and unrecognized.
Set your sights to have 20/20 vision by recognizing the limiting beliefs, thoughts, and opinions you have that prevent you from seeing clearly.   Cast off attachments built from past positions and view a present reality free of a prescription bias.
It's amazing what you can see in the present
when you let go of past views…

These are just a few quick examples of what I would consider non-impeding and often useful filtering control.

It doesn't serve me to notice what types of vehicles are around me, or what time it is at all times, or what clothes my son wears every day. Typically, we would have no real reason to know such things - no attachment, investment, or emotion tied to it - so it remains irrelevant and off the radar.

Yet when it proves to be beneficial to our well-being in some way, the filters drop and awareness flips on - allowing us to "see" in various ways and become cognitive of their existence, sometimes beyond our imagination.

All of this is working together in an effort to protect you - to keep you safe and out of perceived harm's way.

Perfectly logical. In essence, we are "allowed" to be aware of things that would keep us within a certain degree of safety and familiarity; a sort of comfort zone.

Adversely, those things that might remove us from our comfort zone, threaten our sense of safety, or plunge us into areas of the unknown - we pass by with a blind eye.

While this may sound like an ideal scenario on the surface, the thing to look closer at is... What is being deemed harmful? What are we being protected from, and why is it being seen as a threat in the first place?

**We soar only to the heights that we settle for;
what we believe we deserve and are worthy of.**

Note that I didn't say what we THINK.

We can think many things, and that's conscious thought in the moment. What pulls the strings and sets the commands are what we truly BELIEVE, and these beliefs are rooted and deemed to be "true" within the subconscious.

This "standard" belief system we have running allows us to live a reasonably familiar life that we accept as "normal", where we are comfortable and even complacent with both the opportunities and the obstacles that present themselves daily. The subconscious wants to keep us safe, sound, and secure - tied inside our comfort zone - and will use tactics and "truths" that we don't know about or are even aware of to do it.

Don't fight it. Use it to your advantage.
Science has shown that the mind cannot tell the difference between what is real and that which is vividly imagined.

**The wisest gurus throughout the ages have
told us to imagine what it is we want;
to hold in our mind first that which
we wish to hold in our hand.**

The greater clarity of imagination and intensity of belief created for what you want to become a reality, the more you will engage the powers of your subconscious to reveal the opportunities that exist to make it so and utilize your ability to make it happen.
See yourself in ownership of what you want -
engage all of your senses to know its presence.
Go beyond merely imagining achieving it;
experience it as accomplished.
Feeling the reality of it within will set your mind to reeling it in.
In crystal clear clarity, allow your mind to absorb that the life you are living IS comprised of your various dreams, goals, and desires - ALREADY obtained, as real as the ground at your feet.
Do this, and what will shift is that your subconscious will begin seeing the imagined as a part of your comfort zone;
a reality that is and should be.
See, I don't want you to break out of your comfort zone, which can trigger resistance from your subconscious (remember - its program is to protect you and keep you safe and secure).
What I'm saying is that you can change the tack and re-create it to work for you, not against. With the conscious and subconscious rowing in the same direction, the amazing can happen. By having the dreams and goals of your life within your comfort zone - making them an integral part of you feeling safe and protected - *all of your being will move heaven and earth to make it and keep it so.*

This thing to keep in mind:

Merely because there may not be an obvious or direct connection for you between excuses and the various things being shared, it doesn't mean they aren't there.
Comparatively speaking,
                            we are trying to grasp
                    orchestrations of the infinite
            within the comprehension of the finite.

Even though *all* of the tactics and methods of achievement still remain a mystery; there is no "magic" or mysticism to them. Though it might be a bitter pill to swallow, having a life you love, experiencing joy and happiness beyond what you know, and succeeding in every avenue of your life will likely unfold in a manner that seems far less extraordinary than what you may currently hope for. In fact, *it may arrive as you* **expect** *it to.*

The path to the possibilities you create will likely be the result of countless minute, miniscule, and sometimes even mundane things that will occur as ordinary – not extraordinary.
However, a great deal of what is responsible for the groundwork of what is accomplished will not appear on your radar, nor will you recognize it as a piece of the puzzle as a whole because we typically have only a limited conscious realm of reason that we can conceive our solutions to exist within.

In other words, we tend to live our lives believing that we know what the solutions to our problems might look like, and that "believing" limits our view of the possibilities that actually exist. We wait for the answers we want to see and remain blind in our bias and prejudice to answers that don't fit in that familiarity box. With this in play, you can see how rich the fertilizer is for making excuses. You can simply use the excuse of blame for not having the specific solutions that you deem viable for your scenario – which *to you* are the *only* solutions that exist.
Another example would be if you have learned beliefs that lean toward the creation of what you want in life being manifested from thin air with no effort on your part. You will never see the countless opportunities available to you in reality because you will only accept and see the one you imagine and hope for. These people are often those who have developed a belief system that they have tried and failed too many times in the past to think that they can possibly do anything right enough to achieve what they want.

For them, the answer will not be tied to anything they will do themselves, because they see that route as an almost guaranteed failure - and so their efforts often end up being just that. Yes, misplaced beliefs *are* that powerful.

Granted, there are many beliefs, philosophies, and ideologies that have been created over time to explain and fill in the gaps of our understanding and comprehension about the How and Why things happen in life. Ideas and thoughts are designed and created based on the knowledge available at the time – knowledge that is typically believed to be true or reported to be. These ideas were either the best that could be formulated to give answers to the unknown, or the most convenient, beneficial, or believable.
* Side note: "Proof" often comes and goes where profit directs, so it is wise to find the source of it and what the vested interest is for the provider.

Up until more modern times we've lacked the sophistication and technology to really provide any tangible and measurable proof, so we've had to rely mainly on faith. More simply put, the theories and ideas that were best presented and sold are the ones that we believed to be true.
Now, as science continues to unveil and decipher reality, we continue to have breakthroughs in the research of human development, bring further awareness to the workings of mind and body. Facts and proofs are now available where before we had only believable fiction to build our theories with.
I contend that one of the most difficult challenges to face for many people will be to embrace that they have a more direct and reciprocal relationship with themselves and their world than what has traditionally been accepted – and that they have access to a far greater level of control than they can imagine.

At this point, I would be doing you an extreme disservice if I didn't shine some light on this next mention. For those who have strong attachments to their own ideas and beliefs in this area, a few feathers may get ruffled, and I apologize in advance. Once its true depth and breadth is realized and understood, I hope that any residual emotional attachments and mental blocks might be alleviated and revealed for what they are. Until then, there may be a lack in appreciation and conception of how much impact and affect we actually have within our ability and control.

These days, in ever broadening circles, it's not uncommon to hear that everything IS vibration – and vibration is everything when it comes to what happens in life. It would actually be more accurate to say that everything HAS vibration, yet regardless, just what does this mean? How does it impact us?
Outside of its literal, scientific definition, it's often stated as if it were some huge breakthrough - a secret that the mere knowing of is catalyst to create, manifest, and attract every manner of thing into your life that you want. Sound familiar?
I'll broaden the picture a bit.
Most of us, in one fashion or another, have been given explanations that would place the power to change our life and our world outside our reach and in the hands of some universal power - when all along the primary resources are already within our grasp.
I don't mean to be overly repetitive or sound trite, but when I tell you that we - the human Being - is fearfully and wonderfully made, I'm hoping that you will understand that this is far more of a literal statement than some figurative cliche'.
Even today, as they have over the centuries, the greatest minds are still trying to define and explain matters to compare the infinite within the confines of the finite. Similarly, those who do not comprehend that they truly are captain and commander over their life will not accept that they could be "fearfully and wonderfully made". They would not fathom themselves anywhere near the slightly less than angelic stature they are written to be and will always chase their power elsewhere... and away.
It's just that simple, and you can choose to believe it and allow it to work for you or refute it and let it continue working against you.   Either way, it IS always working.
YOU are always working according to beliefs and disbeliefs.

There is a story I heard long ago, and in many ways since, of two wolves - one representing evil, and the other good.
Asked which would win in a fight;
 it is the one that is fed the most.
The more you believe a thing, the more likely you are to make choices and decisions to support that belief. You will feed it.
The opposite is also true. The more you doubt a thing, the more you will make choices and decisions to prove that doubt is warranted and justified. You are feeding the doubt and fear – while starving belief and faith for any other possibility.

The blessing and curse of the matter is that most of this will take place beyond your level of awareness and in ways, as I've said before, that we don't even know exist... yet.

When I was in my twenties, I heard a well-respected entrepreneur say (about excuses) that often they were merely "the skin of a truth stuffed with a lie". What I kept with me, outside of that context, was that there are those things that are not true in their complete content and substance, yet often believed because they contain "the skin of a truth".

We hear and see... many things in this world that we choose to believe because we look at the door and it says "Welcome" in all matter of inviting ways. Ideas and beliefs are dressed in garb and décor that allure and appeal to what we know and trust.

"Go with what you know" is the default mantra of our human nature – a normal way of being for us. Yet behind that door and beneath the costume lies the true content and character within; often incomplete. Often with an agenda. Often with a price tag.

I urge you to always look beyond what at first you see and hear, and simply because things may initially align with your own familiar thoughts and gain your trust - seek the whole truth. Look for the entire picture. Don't be fooled by familiarity.

> *Just because an idea is popular*
> *doesn't mean it's true.*

Similarly, the loudest voices aren't always right.

More often than not, common beliefs of the day are merely the ones that have been the most promoted – especially if declared true by someone of importance, respect, or popularity. (FYI - The earth was always round, regardless of the once popular belief held by both prince and pauper that it was flat.)

Points and dictates are often pulled out of context from all manner of wise script that we would otherwise support and respect – in order to provide legitimacy to the doctrine and ideas being presented for us to believe.

Be aware of your instincts and listen to reason;
do not be blinded by the emotions in the moment.
Don't let your feelings carry you away because something
seems familiar and reminds you of what you already believe.
Superficial securities and false familiarities tend to cause people
to swallow entire ideas, thoughts, teachings, and theories
without proper vetting – simply because that first bite is so
deliciously sweet and inviting. We want to believe it's true!

Hope has filled many a pothole, yet pavement makes a road.
Being the brilliant beings we are, we are masters at
manipulating parts and pieces to finish the puzzles in life.
In those things we want to believe are true, we will gather bits
and pieces of evidence to prove, at least to ourselves, that we
are right in our beliefs. (We do NOT want to be wrong or seen
as wrong – it's a common trait of humanity.) If something
happens in our life that we wanted to happen, or that we didn't
want to happen, we will create a web of connection to our
(conscious) beliefs as to why it did as opposed to following the
actual chain of events that happened to make it so.
Nature abhors a vacuum, and so do we. We don't like the
unknown – it makes us uncomfortable, uneasy; incomplete.
And life is FULL of unknowns, right? BIG ones, little ones,
and all the voids, confusion, and mysteries in between.

Now, more regarding those ideas that are believed by many,
where they came from, and why they are so embraced.

What is the top strategy for business success?
Find a need and fill it!
If you can't do that, **Create** a need and fill it.
And if you can't do that, **Convince** people you know how to,
provide enough proof to satisfy their sensibilities, and
sell them on the sizzle of having their need fulfilled.

We seek answers to our questions, solutions to our problems,
recognition and familiarity to what is unknown, and substance to
fill the voids. When inspired by hope and presented with
something that we believe will meet some manner of need in our
life, we have a tendency to overlook any faults or error.
We fill in the blanks with what we know, and leave it to faith that
anything we don't understand is simply because we lack the
proper enlightenment, wisdom, and understanding.
It's a bit like when we're young and naïve - falling for someone
(in the context of relationships) who we're not real sure about,
but they're cute and seem interested, so we go for it.

Not to offend, but where I see this play out the most is among various religious interpretations and spiritual teachings.

Often an idea is put forth as a "law" or some ancient "secret", supported initially by connecting it to things that we can agree with and makes sense. We're given several examples to review, told that "A" happened because "B" occurred – and led to believe it was all because of "C". We're then told how we can have "C" for ourselves, usually in ways undefinable in earthly terms and only to be seen and experienced on more spiritual realms.

My main point is that it's basic salesmanship when you want to gain agreement to begin with things that we can say "Yes" to and agree on. Psychology tells us that the more times we can get a "Yes" response from people, the more likely they are to agree with what we ultimately want to present.

Almost any manner of falsehood or range of truth can be made believable with the right mixture of ingredients - and it all starts with the skin of a truth. Simply put, begin with a believable truth to win trust, then inject or tie in what you want believed. It is a tried and true method that has worked for centuries. These days, adding the right music, using words that tie in to accepted truths, and giving promise of reward while appealing to our fear of loss are just some tactics that sways people to believe the message being sold. And to really seal the deal and stand apart, the message can be shared by someone who is respected and/or popular - or with a distinctive voice, such as a British accent or very dynamic and energetic vocals.

As an example, many who would promote and have us believe that the "universe" brings to us those things that we want, and that there is some "law" that attracts anything and everything to us. Some go so far as to convince us that taking action toward what we want is proof that we lack faith that it will simply materialize. It's definitely an attractive idea.

If given the choice of belief systems, who wouldn't pick the one that promises and promotes less effort!? Be honest.

Which of these events would YOU buy a ticket for?

Coliseum A:
"The Secret to Having It All Without Doing the Work"
~by (famous published author)

Coliseum B:
"How To Work Hard and Be Smart To Get What You Want"
~by (unknown self-made millionaire)

We both know that Coliseum A would be a sold out show. After all, *most of us think we're smart and work hard* – and look where that got us, right?

These thoughts, theories and ideas that virtually dismiss actions as an important part of the equation and exalt the mind as an ultimate magnet to our dreams and desires often resonate with those who aren't aware of nor understand their own potential and power as a human being. And that's... all of us, to a degree. Truly.
To people who feel like they don't have control over their life, in their eyes, the ability to have more or be more *must* come from some outside source - not as a result of their own doing or ability. Yet throughout history, weaving through science, spirituality, religions, and reality – it has been revealed that *action* is actually the greatest testament to one's faith and belief. **BOTH are crucial**... and whether you're aware of it or not - each is taking place at levels known and unknown to you.

IF the understanding was present to how much control, contact, connection, and communication there was between the world within us and the world around us, we could better see the deficiencies of these incomplete yet popular doctrines.

Again, there is enough "truth" to them as to be believable by many very intelligent people, and if they didn't contain at least some beneficial instruction or helpful remedy, they would have faded away long ago as a fad. Far from saying we should throw out the baby with the bathwater, I'm suggesting that incomplete teachings can actually limit our ability and dampen our potential. Though there may initially be good intent in the beginning, we are often sent on paths for the sake *of* the path and to perpetuate the travel of it at a profit for others, rather than producing positive results and breakthroughs in our own life.

Though volumes more could be said about this, it isn't my intention to go further in depth on this topic. It is being mentioned because it is relevant to the degree that often we *do* feel as though things are out of our control, and *this perceived lack of control* **becomes an excuse** expressed in many ways.

For many, no matter how hard they try, it feels like nothing works, and they assume and assert that the only way to get what they want in life is out of their hands and beyond their control. They believe that there must be a power outside of themselves that makes things happen, and they turn their time and attention to chasing a "magic" that will bring what they want to them. Many shortsighted teachings would have people believe that what they want in life *should* come with ease and little effort, and it is merely their lack of faith and belief that prevent them from having it accordingly. Hard work = wrong. In short, what ends up happening is that we make excuses for why we don't pursue various opportunities because they don't look "spiritual" or "enlightened" enough.

To state it more bluntly, if it looks like work might be involved, we pass it by – believing it cannot be part of *OUR* divinely anointed plan, and time after time, opportunity after opportunity, the best solutions remain blind to our closed mind.

This next piece may as well be said now, and I ask that you set any preconceived notions aside about it so you can hear me. Deal?

Here is the missing link for those people who think that getting what they want is all about action
           - and those who think it's all about belief.

You can put all the action you want forth, but without adequate faith and belief, you will find yourself constantly faltering.

You can believe all you want and chant til the cows come home, but until you *move* and *ACT* in faith – you will live in frustration.

So, for the realist, the open-minded, the optimist, and even the pessimist - I'd like to help bridge a gap between science and this spirituality. Again, keep in mind that, comparatively speaking, we're trying to define the infinite within the confines of the finite. (Remember the example from earlier, how the 18,000 bathtubs full of water - 660,000 gallons - compares to the 1 quart?)

When you have set your deepest beliefs to be in the place where your comfort zone is and your subconscious has equated where you are "supposed" to be within these beliefs; your potential resources are multiplied by over 2,640,000 times what you thought possible. Instead of only having 1 quart (conscious) of potential, possibility, and opportunity to plot, plan, and execute your dreams, goals, and desires - you now have over 2,640,000 quarts ready to do your bidding (subconscious).

At this point, I'm dying to geek out and go into numerous "Hows" and "Whys" that, if understood and embraced, might completely change your concept of everything you know, and everything you don't. I'm going to do my best to restrain myself. After all, we didn't sign up for that. Excuses. FOCUS!

Various organizations utilize simulations as a way to train people. For example, let's us a flight simulator used to train Air Force pilots. The simulator is going to resemble an actual cockpit, with controls, and a screen. A computer program will run various real-life scenarios, and according to the actions/reactions of the pilot within the simulation (interaction within the program), the "mission" plays out accordingly. The simulation will appear very familiar - a combination of scenery, terrain, other aircraft, possibly even a few birds; everything that a pilot flying an aircraft might encounter and experience is designed within the program, in surround sound and high-resolution video in the advanced units. Within the simulation - you are a pilot, and you have the ability to control what a pilot can control within it.

Your subconscious is acting director over the show that is your life; it is the software designer/developer of the simulation of your conscious reality. You are the pilot in this simulation; therefore, the simulator is running a program for a pilot.

At any point, to some degree or another, everything the pilot sees, hears, and "experiences" is familiar to a pilot.
The pilot is not suddenly dropped into a lion cage at a zoo in their simulation. The pilot does not turn their controller to the right and suddenly find themself looking into the window of a flower shop. They will see those things that would be in an acceptable range of normal to see for a pilot – within their place, expected position, and scope of conscious possibility.

The excuses you come up with in life and the
underlying reasons you come up with them
are born out of the defense of
who you believe yourself to be
and within the program created to confine
you inside of that reality for protection.

Even while in your mother's womb, the subconscious of You has been gathering data with which to create a simulation of Life. From all of your experiences, all your senses, surroundings, and environment - your subconscious has also built the identity of You; creating the role you are to play within the simulation.

The storyline of your Life follows the story, and you are shown the stage - complete with a supporting cast, and backdrops - by what your mind filters out and by what it brings awareness to.

As we grow older, experience adds to experience, and additional input is taken into the equation of roles you can play; yet intact remains the identity and familiarity of You. Things and events happen, and we react with a familiar way of being to them.

Day by day, our lives play out a recording of our yesterdays in a familiar array of habits, customs, and tasks that meet the expectations of the mind and fall within the parameters of the simulation program. Note that I did not include wants and desires. For many, not fulfilling our wants and desires IS the deeper expectation of the mind and a large part of what is our familiar. This is all carried out in part by means we still have only limited understanding of, and in its entirety, we may never fully comprehend or reach with our conscious sense.

One way to depict the "How" this all might unfold in our reality (in finite terms) would be to reverse engineer what's often referred to as the "butterfly effect".

Dictionary.com defines it as this:

"butterfly effect
Noun
a cumulatively large effect that a very small natural force may produce over a period of time."

Wikipedia explains it better this way;

"the butterfly effect is the sensitive dependence on initial conditions in which a small change in one state of a deterministic nonlinear system can result in large differences in a later state. ... A very small change in initial conditions had created a significantly different outcome."

Another way to relay the concept would be to dissect a process from the end result backward, tracking down and taking into consideration *every* element of influence, force, and development while discovering what they had in common, in relation, and in cohesion with one another, that allowed for the orchestration of the final outcome.

If given enough time, one could make connection after connection to the path that eventually led us to where we are. With our sensory abilities constantly feeding the mind with input, and the subconscious filing, filtering, and processing of it to support its primary purpose and objective – we communicate with and to our own capabilities to bring substance to the unseen. Again, it isn't the result of some secret, mystical magic, or set of contrived laws, but rather networking at levels we have only scratched the surface of understanding and identifying.

For example, say we wanted to increase our income. Beyond the more obvious steps, such as (for example) speaking with a potential partner in a business venture, seeking higher education, or working harder and smarter in a job – consider those things *not* so observed up *to* that point.

Every minute movement of our body and being – each word uttered and muttered under our breath; everything transmitted, transferred, received and perceived, translated, and interpreted. And this is just the start of what WE are doing to determine and cause an outcome; how WE are effecting a result.

For our conscious mind to research and discover all of the factors involved in such an elaborate construct would be a feat no Sherlock Holmes, Stephen Hawking, or Albert Einstein would dare even on their best day and given a thousand lifetimes.

When your subconscious sets out to "put you in your place", so-to-speak, you won't be able to conceptualize or connect all the dots that made it possible.

What it might look like on the outside (as a positive example) is this; You will do what you know to do, and take actions you think will achieve the results you want. Along the way, you may have revelations, discover additional resources, have new ideas, and possibly even find others who will contribute to the process. Opportunities will be present, maybe a lucky break or two or three, and regardless of the hits and misses - the desired end result is achieved. Long story short, you end up being in the place of having what it was you believed you could have and create in and for your life.
Guess what?
It wasn't a result of that "quart" of knowledge, ability, or skill that you possessed; it was the ebbing flood of 660,000 gallons of Knowing and affecting churning in the background.
Your subconscious will orchestrate your thoughts and actions, design plans of which you are unaware, and have you interact with and within your world in ways that you cannot consciously comprehend, notice, or even suspect would play a role.

The kicker is, the same brain that can break us free from our condition and circumstance - creating miraculous results - has also been chaining us to limiting beliefs throughout our life, keeping us in an accepted state of feeling safe and sound in what we know and are comfortable in.
PLEASE NOTE that I did not say to "keep us in comfort".
You and I both know people who live in situations that are just... awful, and we can't understand why they won't do something about it. Their life is anything but comfortable!
However, in their mind - regardless of how it might look - this is what they know. It is what they are comfortable with, believe they deserve, and they will continue to be cause in creating their life to perpetuate it. Of course, there will always be excuses for it that sound reasonable and seem rational.

Your life, right now - as good or as bad as it is,
is also operating at an accepted level of "comfort".
And, as you may have guessed by now, you've had
reasons and made excuses for it all that make sense.
Hopefully you are beginning to realize that you have
unknowingly been far more instrumental for where
you are in your life than you could have ever imagined.

Knowing this, that you *have* been affecting and effecting your life up until this point, is key to your being able to shape your future to look more like you want it.
Because now you know you have been.
You simply weren't aware of it.

Understandably, the subject of thought and how to intentionally use our mind to develop the life we want isn't taught in any traditional K-12 school setting that I am aware, as of the year 2020. It is my hope that as awareness grows on the subject, the demand for an educational system dedicated to teaching children essential life skills with the intention of having them understand their individual potential will evolve.

The same cookie-cutter subjects that have been taught for generations have long outlived their usefulness in a free-thinking society so far beyond the industrial revolution.

I mention this because for many, our foundation of education is based upon a very limited set of fundamentals and beliefs. Until children are taught to realize their potential and ability to create the life they want, they will rarely accept or embrace a sense of personal responsibility for their life.

They will grow up feeling entitled to what they want -
expecting it to be given to them, rather than
knowing or appreciating that it is theirs to earn.
Yet with this enabling disempowerment, they would continually blame others for their circumstances, feeling powerless and out of control to change things in their life.
That's what happens when all manner of provision is simply given, and every effort is taken to make a person feel good rather than giving them the tools and training to take care of their own mental, physical, and emotional needs.

One doesn't have to look far to see the rampant evidence of this in today's society, yet I remain hopeful that we can stem this destructive mindset and learned attitude.

And yes, this actually applies to children of all ages;
and it matters from birth to final breath...

Consider this:

Your mind has told you
and sold you on the idea that,
  what you think and believe in
  is enlightened and progressive,
  rather than impractical and unsustainable.

And sometimes, it turns those around -
telling you and selling you on the idea that,
  what you think and believe in
  is impractical and unsustainable,
  rather than enlightened and progressive.

Keep in mind that you will be led
to where you believe you belong,
so the real secret is "make believe".
Make yourself believe that
you belong where you want to be,
and watch what is unraveled and
revealed in the travels of your Life.

Do not lose sight of this:

Though we are fearfully and wonderfully made -
      our workings are fragile and susceptible to influence.

To the extreme degree that we are being influenced,
now more than ever it is important to be intentional,
directional, conscious and coherent about what we *can*
do to control our lives. Either **we** will be in control,
or by default allow ourselves to *be* controlled by an
environment and circumstances not of our design.

Repeating the rhetoric of false reality

When I tell you that science is still discovering ways in which we receive input - how the human being is a receptor of information beyond what can be seen, heard, or felt - I'm only scratching the surface. *Our understanding in and of most of what we know is at the mercy of the tools and instruments we have to detect, dissect, and measure with - and the interpretation of it by what we consciously know or allow others to convince us of as true.* Until we have the ability to "see" everything there is that is - we must work with what we know as it presents itself. Speaking of seeing, for example, the discovery was made not long ago that our bodies have an ability to "see" light, independent of our eyes. This begs the question - What other sensory receptors, currently unknown, might be lurking within our bodies - out of "sight", yet not out of (conscious) mind?

Let's bridge over to hearing as "seeing". Just as bats emit sounds as a part of their "radar" to locate objects, did you know humans also have this ability? As you can imagine, those who have been found to utilize this skill were also visually deprived (blind) - yet it can be learned to a degree by those who aren't. This begs the question; since we know this is possible, and that the brain / nervous system has the capability to achieve this on a conscious level - is it possible that a similar function is in play beneath our awareness?

What other modes of sensory do we have within us that is not tied to any part of consciousness, yet employed in harmony with the subconscious? In what other ways might there be present, yet unseen systems and circuits designed to sense and interact with our surroundings and environment – beneath the radar of conscious? Is it unbelievable to presume that we may even be communicating with others on a level completely out of the realm of conscious awareness? Surely, you've met people who you have an uneasy feeling about, yet just can't seem to figure out why, right? What if there is communication taking place – the sending and receiving of information on levels tied only to the neural network of the subconscious mind, and armed with this data your subconscious is trying to alert the conscious You to a potential danger? After all, that IS a subconscious directive, remember?

Currently, our explanations of existence border on the mystical, yet it's only a matter of time before science will further perceive and penetrate the veil of mystery that is the human Being.

Back to the less obscure and relevant.

Did you know that we "hear" more than what we are hearing? Though our conscious can discern sound within a certain frequency range, our auditory ability to sense soundwaves goes beyond that. Cats and dogs, for example, can hear sounds that are at a higher frequency than we can, while elephants can hear sounds that are lower than we can hear. Subliminal sound technologies have existed for quite some time, both as a means of suggestive manipulation as well as all out weaponization. Our subconscious is "hearing" far more than our conscious. Given that our environment - including other human beings - emit soundwaves of varying frequencies, is it not also possible there might be a level of communication or interpreting happening that we are not aware of?

We know that our brain and body creates and is controlled by electrical impulses and signals. In labs and in life we have found external influence to change the operation and function of the body - even the transformation of tissue itself - outside of its intended design.

The million-dollar question is; how much is our environment impacting our internal chemical and electromagnetic control systems? The billion-dollar question is; how much influence do our internal chemical and electromagnetic functions have on the world around us and with others?

The reality is not IF in either scenario, but to what extent.

Are you beginning to see how it is that what you are capable of and what you think you can do are on very different realms?

With all of the stimuli that exists at our fingertips and bombards us every day, the constant filtering, organizing, and prioritizing of it all can wear us down - literally. Both focus AND filtering of input - sorting the things our conscious mind will and won't be allowed to see - takes energy, and a tired brain often takes the easy way out and the path of least resistance.

Excuses are many times that easier path.

To make matters worse, there is a TON of garbage being slung our way that we need to deal with, and we're taking in trash not only from what we eat and drink, but what we see, hear, and are exposed to beyond our conscious ability to detect.

It's going in, and it's taking a toll; physically and mentally.

Especially in America, there is far more in our environment to be dealt with by our mind and body than ever before, and unfortunately the advancement of civilization and the modernizing of our culture has come at a steep cost. To those who stand to gain from it, as long as appearances are kept in check and detrimental impact concealed, the substance beneath, or lack thereof, has been of little concern.

I've covered a good deal of this in other books, but in being mindful of our longing to know *Why*, I feel compelled to share the following:

When it comes to thinking straight, we're a long way from stepping out onto a level playing field. The body supports and nourishes the brain - our mind - however you look at it. They are connected. What goes into our body - in any manner - ultimately affects the mind.

With that in mind, know that your diet impacts how you think and feel for many reasons and on many levels, and plays a large role in the creation of excuses in your life.

When I was a kid, I heard the phrase "You are what you eat". You may have heard it, too. Those 5 words hold a deeper truth than any of us knew when we were kids, similar to "Garbage in, garbage out".

Simply because something is commonly accepted as "food" does not mean it provides adequate sustenance for your body. A great deal of the "food" that you find in the grocery stores is fraudulent at best, requiring an extraneous amount of energy for our bodies to digest and filter through in an effort to extract any beneficial nutrition.

The popular foods being consumed in our society come from a long line of chemically altered and engineered sources. This doesn't just apply to synthetic creations, either. Not even the produce aisles are safe from the bastardization of our food supply, with our animal and plant-based foods being seriously deficient in both vitamin and mineral content. In addition, they also contain toxic compounds left behind from fertilizing, weed killers, and insecticides, not to mention the impact that genetically modified organisms (GMOs) have on the ecosystem that we are a part of. In a nutshell, generations of "advanced" growing and farming practices have yielded nutrient retarded crops, diluted of their natural minerals, vitamins, proteins, and crucial amino acids – while at the same time contaminating us with a laundry list of residual byproducts that would bear the badge of a skull and crossbones.

Aside from digging in to what you can eat that's actually good for you, do yourself a HUGE favor and read up on foods that are not only good for the body, but also help nourish the brain. Don't make an excuse why you won't,
why you don't, or why you can't.
Your "Why not" is just another echo of excuses
gone by to keep you inside a "good enough" life.
News flash: "Good enough", when it comes to your health, usually ends in "I wish I had" or "If only I'd" statements of regret uttered years down the road - when it's too late and the damage has been done.
Hospitals and cemeteries are filled with people who believed "good enough" would allow them to live a long, happy, healthy life. I happen to think you deserve better than regret and suffering - and so do your friends and family.

On top of what we consume, every day, our bodies have to deal various pollutants in the air, and toxins in our water, such as chlorine, lead, fluoride, and arsenic, in addition to the poisonous chemicals found in fertilizers, weed killers, and insecticides that find their way back into our water supply.
In short, we're consuming a lot of what is bad for us,
and very little of what is good. Speaking of good –
2 easy things you can start doing now if want to
be proactive in regaining more clarity of thought:

1) Eat a *lot* of leafy green vegetables, and include fruit, nuts, and fish high in Omega 3s in your diet.
2) Drink adequate water for your body weight (average = 8 glasses a day), adding lemon juice (1/2 lemon) to *at least* your morning glass of (warm) water. If half your daily water intake is lemon infused, your brain AND body will benefit greatly.

You must know that the common diet in this country is loaded with foods that interfere with our ability to think clearly, and **when we can't think straight,** *it's easier to make excuses*. Let's say that again in a different way: *the average person is handicapped in their cognitive abilities as a result of the food they eat,* **and it is their normal way of thinking.**

If a child were born with 20/200 vision, how would life occur to that child growing up? Normal. They would have to stand 20 feet away from things to see them clearly where a person with standard eyesight could see them clearly from 200 feet away. Let that child grow up without doing anything to improve their eyesight, and more importantly, have the child remain unaware that anything at all was wrong with their eyesight, and that child would be oblivious to any "handicap" or "impairment".

They would do things to the best of their ability, never knowing they were living a life so blurred and fogged over. They could see what they could see, and act & react accordingly.

Now, what if you came over and told them that if they were to wear a pair of lenses over their eyes they would be able to fix their impaired vision? Their first response might be along the lines of "What do you mean '*impaired* vision'?
What's wrong with the way I see now? I can see fine!"

I want you to really wrap your head around that scenario.
You are in essence telling someone that they are not seeing things clearly when, in their eyes, they've been managing just fine and seeing things the way they were meant to be seen.
You are trying to convince someone that the way they have been seeing the world their entire life is WRONG.

Incidentally, (a bit of aside here) if you haven't experienced this yourself by now, allow me to break the news gently.
When you suggest to people that something they are doing in their life is somehow "wrong", they can get… testy.
To most people (especially if you try to shed light on darker areas), their life is fine – regardless of what challenges they may have gone through or are going through now.
They may not like aspects of their life, but it's fine really.
It's just the way things are.
If you go and suggest that they might actually be a bit oblivious to those things that are preventing them from living a better life, be prepared for a degree of blowback. It's just human nature.

We're only human, right? We get defensive when "attacked" in some manner – whether it's real or simply perceived.
Remember what I said earlier about the subconscious wanting to protect us from perceived harm?
Well, it's going to give us some very intelligent responses, reasons, and excuses to try and convince us and anyone else that we are OK where we are and that we can see just fine.
As a matter-of-fact, clearly YOU are just being judgmental for suggesting that they aren't "right" in some way.
After all, who made you God?!?
Besides, your life isn't perfect and you aren't "All that".
Best to keep your piety and righteous opinions to yourself, thank you very much! And next time we want any of your "Holier than Thou" words of advice and superiority, we'll call you – OK?

Trust me – your subconscious can find all of the best excuses, triggers, and hot buttons it needs to manipulate you and everyone around you to keep you in your "place".

Now, back to our 20/200 visionary scenario.
Let's call her Cecelia.
What if for a moment she was at least open to the suggestion that having the lenses over her eyes might at least show her something that might be... different than what she may currently see. If for no other reason than to satisfy curiosity, or even prove us wrong – what if she put the lenses on?
She would see things around her that she could not see without them on, and the things around her could be seen more clearly.

It doesn't take rocket scientist to see how that could impact her world and open up possibilities that were not even on the radar.
After all, you don't know what you don't know – and if all you know is blurry vision and sailing through life in a fog;
 ~you wouldn't even have a concept of what clear is.
You wouldn't recognize it for what it was;
 the absence of what stands in the way
 of your ability to see what is really there.

So, let me go back to the very basic and fundamental truth that led us here: **What you put in your mouth matters**.

Let me repeat that.
What you put in your mouth matters.

For someone who already has challenges or sensitivities related to brain function, it can be an invisible prison from which they cannot break free. They can't see the bars. They often have no association between mental dysfunction and diet. Additionally, most people in this situation crave the very things that keep them from thinking clearly. These commonplace comfort foods have become the unconscious drug of choice for many.

It should be no surprise that we are so easily swayed by our subtle addictions, though. We have become slaves to our taste buds and convinced that we should base our decisions on what feels good (looks good, smells good, tastes good, etc.) – not be wrapped up in whether it's actually good for us or not.

Billions of dollars are spent each year trying to convince us to buy goods and services, food and other consumables especially, NOT because they are good for us – but because it's profitable to have a customer base that is hooked on what you're offering. There are businesses and various enterprises that
exist solely for the sake of selling you on the sizzle.

From beef to belief systems, we're being sold a
bill of goods whose priority isn't to be good for us,
but to be profitable for those peddling the product.

And yes, we moved way beyond the farm on this topic, but awareness is one of our greatest assets in life, so it had to be said. "Ignorance is bliss" might be a cute saying, but when it comes to your body and mind, being naïve about what goes in to both will bring you a very frustrating level of existence filled with all manner of excuses for your "settle for" life. Science has long been uncovering the facts and discovering the forces that create disharmony in the body and dysfunction of the mind, revealing (among other things) that the connection between the gut and the brain can no longer be ignored.

So, for now – let's just agree to stop being so gullible when it comes to what we put in our mouth, shall we?

Stop being fooled by the latest fads and falling for the "sizzle" of the newest craze that promises the moon.

Don't allow what's popular to prey on your well-being, and just say "NO!" to being casual about what goes in your body & brain.

Sound good?

One more thing I am compelled to share again with you. Merely because there may not be an obvious or direct connection for you between excuses and various things mentioned in this book *doesn't mean they aren't there.*

Remember, in comparison; **we are trying to grasp orchestrations of the infinite within the comprehension of the finite**.

NOTES:
(Those things that keep popping into my head that I know I should write down yet let the excuse "I'll remember" win out)

_____

(I'm taking the liberty to jot one down for you)
When you FEEL good and when you FEEL healthy - you're going to make healthier decisions and better choices for your life.

We're going to be moving on to areas that, though they affect us, are often not on the "radar" of things that the average person would be aware of to any great degree.

For example, wireless technologies, whether we personally use them or not, have grown to the extent that their reach is virtually inescapable, yet still their effect on both the mind and body remains publicly unknown for the most part, in spite of research and evidence clearly showing the detrimental impact and potential harm they can cause.

Electromagnetic frequencies emitted by appliances, machinery, technology, and telecommunications continue to damage cells, impede brain development, and diminish proper function within the nervous system. Additionally, our feelings, emotions, and moods can be altered - and even the very DNA upon which we are made stands at risk of being corrupted.

Remember, our bodies, to varying degrees, are antennae themselves - capable of both sending AND receiving signals, and therefore susceptible to exterior manipulation. This is why I've had concern over the 5G telecommunications technology that has been in various stages of implementation. It is public information, though concealed rather than promoted, that even the pre-existing platforms have had their own levels of detriment to the brain and body. At the levels that 5G has been approved of and set in place - many times that of previous generations - the nature and algorithm of signals being sent has been found to impact and impair the normal function of the mind and body. It is also being discovered, after-the-fact, that various elements and chemicals already present or introduced into the body can further accentuate these negative effects.

Inconvenient information, to say the least.

Still, we as a population are used to living with the hazards of a modern world; the cost of a "civilized" society. We've paid and continue to pay a price for it - we're just never told the ultimate cost, and the bill usually comes due decades late.

Knowing that our minds operate in a symmetry of chemical and electromagnetic means, concluding that our thoughts and actions are affected and influenced by all of these things is a given. How well we are able to adapt and function in spite of them depends on how well we can push back and defend against their disruption and corruption to our being.

Our ability to be naturally "grounded" and dissipate the negative effects of these nearly inescapable technologies is all but lost in our "civilized" society. Never before have we been so isolated and insulated from being able to discharge against the constant buildup of free radicals and "ground" ourselves (literally).

Being naive to the existence of these things will not defer their effect, just as not believing in gravity doesn't mean you will fly.

The better you can take care of your physical well-being and push back against the forces that would deteriorate it, the easier it will be for it to support your mental well-being. Jump starting your mental state to a point where it makes putting your physical well-being a priority is the first step, otherwise you will continually fall back on unhealthy ways of living.

On the topic of unhealthy ways of living, I'd be cheating you greatly if I didn't cover this next subject. Of course, I've got to risk stepping on a few toes again, because there are those who believe that what they see and hear won't affect them because they "know better" and understand the difference between entertainment and reality. Many people would try to convince us that the music we listen to and what we watch doesn't really matter - that it's no big deal. Even before I began studying human behavior over 30 years ago, it's always been difficult for me to imagine that anyone would believe that it doesn't impact or affect us. Again, not believing in gravity won't save us from falling off the cliff, just as saying that the cliff itself only exists in our mind will not soften the rocky landing below.
(More on this subject later).
In today's world, with the ease of access to information that we have at our fingertips, it continues to boggle my mind that we haven't made the common sense connection that what we see and hear via music and media sends a message. These messages are being transferred to the brain, where the programming of the mind takes place – like it or not.
And yes, this has everything to do with excuses in our life – because our beliefs and "truths" are formed based on the data that comes into our mind, whether consciously aware or not.

So, I'll just jump right in.
For you "music" lovers - do you listen to the words in what you hear? (Your subconscious is listening to every word, FYI) Are they giving you instruction on how to live an empowered life? Is what you listen to sending positive messages on how to treat others and yourself? Are you being encouraged to care about yourself and others? Are the words telling you that you are more than enough to achieve what you want? Are the lyrics heard in a typical day empowering and telling you that you are responsible for your life, or do they say you have no control and blame some part of society for your problems?
Are you mindful to the messages in the music,
or do you simply allow the words to slip by unnoticed?

Music, as many are aware, stimulates and opens up the brain, causing it to be more receptive, relaxed and open to suggestion. Any message within the music more easily passes through our conscious mind and is driven into the subconscious.
Some people have thought me to be overly concerned with certain types of music and my "dislike" of certain songs.
For the most part it's been easy for me to just say; "garbage in, garbage out", and hope they see the simplicity within that answer rather than ask them to dig into the science that reveals why pouring trash into their head isn't a good idea.

If you listen to the majority of "popular" music that is played in our society, you might understand why most of it is detrimental to the positive growth of your mental state and against the belief that you are cause in your life. So much of it is angry, divisive, victimizing, self-focused, incredibly demeaning - especially to women - and repeats a dogma of how the world and those in it are not fair. It frequently calls you out as a victim, tells you to "get even", and that what matters most is how you feel.
THAT is the kind of garbage that is being stuffed deep into our minds. I'm being conservative here, and as usual, candy coating things a bit more than I should. But I really hope you get this.
And here's the reason it's so important; the messages in music impress far more than simply words spoken.
I won't go into the science of it, but music "lights up" more of the brain than any other single input method.
When you listen to music, you are engaging far more of the brain than if you were merely listening to someone speaking - and what is going into your ears and into your brain when the music plays has a much greater reach and impact.

Being selective about the music in your life can play a HUGE part in your conscious and subconscious thought process, which in turn factors into the excuses you will or will not make.
It can be one more brick in the wall of your life that keeps you from what you want, or if you use it wisely, part of the bridge that connects you to it.
The other relevant and prevalent area I've got to add to this is what you take in visually. I'm just going to cut to the chase on this one; television shows, movies, videos, and video games to name the most common. Let's just call it screen time.
I know - in a few minutes the only people left reading this are going to be you, me, and a handful of die-hards who are actually serious about getting control over their life instead of hung up over comments made about the music & TV they like.
(I like cheesecake, but there's really nothing in it that's good for me and far too much that's bad – even if it does go down the gullet deliciously.)

Remember when I said (as have the greatest minds have shared for decades) that the mind cannot tell the difference between what is real and that which is vividly imagined?
At no other time in history are we being exposed to more vivid imagery than today. The technology to bring to the screen of choice high resolution and high definition "reality" is absolutely incredible. And don't toy with me - we both know what's popular on the screens being watched by the majority of households. Too much of it shows violence on every level, sexual deviations too many to keep track of, scandal, promiscuity; you name the depravity, it's being made to be just another walk in the park - paraded in front of us and perpetrated as normal and acceptable. We tell ourselves that we know it's not real, it's just "entertainment". Of course, that's our 1 quart of water talking, meanwhile our 660,000 gallons are soaking it up and adding it to our Being as a measure of truth.
All of that garbage is now being used in the equation of how you process and see Life - regardless of what you tell yourself.
I know, I'm a being a buzzkill here - especially when I tell you that by adding music (which most TV shows & movies do) to the visual experience it's being driven even further and deeper into your mind. And don't get me started on the ads and commercials, where essentially you are told that you're either somehow "less than" without their product, or how you would be so much better with it. The basic business model of "Find a need and fill it" has become "Create a need and fill it" - and fortunes have been spent convincing you of and creating the "needs" that you need filled.

PARENTS:
If you have kids who play video games,
think long and hard on this again:

***the mind cannot tell the difference between
what is real and that which is vividly imagined.***

If you ever wanted to program a child to devalue human life and diminish personal responsibility, let them play the more popular video games on the market. A vast majority of them, in one way or another, are designed to provide a reward for causing death and destruction - with incredibly realistic detail and graphics. It's been this way for decades.
Now, many would deny that this type of "entertainment" interaction is detrimental and say that it doesn't affect their minds. That's completely understandable. It's the society we live in. I get it. We, as adults, by now have had our own fair share of immersion into a twisted sense of reality, thanks in great part to a largely agenda driven mainstream media and entertainment industry.
That is a story for another time.
Just know that for children of all ages (this includes you, my Friend), their "down time" and entertainment is playing a part in their development and how they think and feel about themselves and the rest of the world.

Boiled down, you, me; WE are being desensitized
to the value of... well, the value of values, really.
The value of life is being eroded; yours and of others,
as is the value of morals, the value of right and wrong,
the value of peace, love, honor, appreciation, commitment, perseverance, integrity, respect, patience, and trust.
The value of believing that each of us is fearfully and wonderfully made, worthy of the best - and giving our best - in the world that we live in; all of these and more continue to be thrown by the wayside and treated with indifference and even contempt.

Don't shoot the messenger.
Simply understand that there are things you can add to your life that would improve it, just as there are things that you could remove that would make a positive difference.

If you're like most people, you have a lot of catching up to do in both of these areas. Also like most people, you may not believe that you do, and have collected enough excuses to convince you not to rock the boat too much.

Incidentally, before I leave the subject of screens - there are many other negatively impacting effects of screen time that I haven't even touched on. Since the average person spends about 10 hours a day interacting with them, which is more than half your waking hours, I hope you'll find it important enough to explore them and make positive shifts in this area.

Now, allow me a moment of candid intervention, if you will.

If it is your intent to simply toy with the idea of only changing a few things in your life, but not do anything too drastic or severe - I've got to ask you; What else is so important?
What is your excuse for not wanting to step up
to the plate and hit a home run for your Life?
For the love of grape juice,
you've got one run
on this wonderful world;
No trials, no rehearsals, no practice runs -
this isn't drill; we march NOW!

Your decisions and direction don't need to be popular, and you don't need permission for your mission!

Let me sum up something I heard when I was
still in my early twenties, because in the end,
we will do what we want when we want to bad enough:

**To have what most people don't,
do what most people won't.**

It's that simple.

I had to break this out and elaborate on it further because there is something that you listen to more often and has a greater impact on your life than any speaker or screen.

It's you.

Have you ever heard of the 80/20 rule?
It basically says that 80% of your results come from 20% of your efforts. Well, it just so happens that roughly 80% of our self-talk is negative.
Sure, it may just be a coincidence, but it's no wonder we live our lives so beneath our potential when our self-talk is running positive only 20% of the time.

It shouldn't be called "self-talk", because what we are ultimately doing is self-teaching, self-training, and self-programming ourselves to keep them real. Our conscious use of words is commanding the subconscious to be cause in the circumstances that support our stated belief.
For example, when you say "No matter what I do, it's not good enough", you are setting a directive for your subconscious to insure that, whatever your intentions, your results will fall short of satisfaction.
As I alluded to earlier, the resourcefulness and reach of the subconscious to influence and impact our lives is beyond comprehension. You won't even be aware of all the different ways and processes that will be involved in making sure that you will receive "proof" (such as in this example) that no matter what you do, it won't be good enough.
Here are some more examples that may sound familiar to you, and they're just the tip of the iceberg that is the negative self-talk programming your life.
Keep in mind that, whether you are saying these types of things to others or yourself, the first person who hears them is YOU. If you are saying these things to other people, now you have them believing this "truth" and their interactions will join in to support the belief.

Examples:

It's no use
I don't care
I can't do it
I'm too busy
I'm so stupid
Nothing works
I always do this
I always do that
I'm such a retard
I never have time
I get ignored a lot
I'm afraid of flying
I always forget that
I never do that right
I always get teased
I get sick all the time
I'm not good at math
I'm not good at sales
I'm just not that smart
I'm not a good speller
Animals don't like me
I'm not good with kids
When it rains, it pours
I always do that wrong
I always get ripped off
I don't do well on tests
I'm not good with people
I can never catch a break
They probably don't like me
I can't see myself doing that
My car always breaks down
I always get treated like crap
That won't make a difference
If it's not one thing, it's another
I big house is too much hassle
I can never seem to get ahead
Everything I eat goes to my hips
They always get my order wrong
I always get the raw end of the deal
No matter what I do, it's not good enough
I always do terrible on these kinds of tests
Wealthy people always have so many problems
No matter how hard I try, I always (insert failure HERE)
I always forget to empty my pockets before I do laundry

I never remember to take my vitamins in the morning
I always run out of money before I run out of month
He/She would never go for someone like me
I wouldn't survive working over 8 hours a day
If it wasn't for bad luck, I'd have no luck at all
I always get carsick when I read in the car
I can't function without 8 hours of sleep
I always get those switched around
People never take me seriously
I can never seem to lose weight
There's no way I can afford that
Nothing ever works out for me
I'll never be able to afford that
I always get lost when I drive
At this rate, I'll never make it
They always make fun of me
People always do that to me
My family always judges me
I'll never be able to do that
I can never remember that
They don't care about me
I never have enough time
I'll try, but I doubt it'll work
Cancer runs in my family
I never have time for that
I can never get that right
It doesn't matter anyway
They'll never go for that
They never listen to me
I always forget my keys
I doubt they'll call back
I always burn the toast
I always screw that up
It's not going to work
I'm not good at that
I always lose things
I suck at doing that
I'm not very strong
Nothing I try helps
I'm such an idiot
I can't help it
It's too late

I'd be shocked if you didn't have a "But..." to at least one of these statements, so before you begin to negate the entire point based on an excuse (which we can be very good at doing) - listen carefully.
Pick anything on this list. The more you say it, the more often it will occur - not because you are consciously creating it to happen, but because you are unknowingly causing it to persist by your expectation and speaking.

Throughout the ages, the wisest have understood the power of our words. From King Solomon to William Shakespeare, and Jesus Christ to Deepak Chopra - words of wisdom have been shared in many ways that we might harness the power of our tongue. This Chinese proverb sums it up well:
"A tongue may weigh little but it can crush a man."
This goes for our words to others,
yet more importantly to ourselves.

The negative self-talk that runs through your brain is detrimental to your well-being, yet add to it the impact and affect on your life when those words escape your mouth.

When you tell yourself or someone else something like;
"I can never seem to get ahead" - you believe it,
and that statement said in belief sets the stage for what your subconscious is to maintain as true.
Guess what your mind will NOT allow you to see?
Opportunities that might cause you to get ahead.
Guess what your mind WILL allow you to see? More and more evidence that would prove you just can't seem to get ahead. Your subconscious will brilliantly assist you in making just enough poor decisions to thwart even your best efforts to get ahead. As long as your dialogue continues to be filled with predictions of failure and hopelessness, you will continue to receive and achieve more of what you don't want.
And, until you comprehend how much power and control you really have over your life - you'll never see the connection nor realize or believe that you are the one causing it.

Confucius say;
 "Without knowing the force of words,
   it is impossible to know more."
(Literally, he said that... only in Chinese), and take it from Sigmund Freud himself, considered the father of psychoanalysis; "Words have a magical power. They can either bring
 the greatest happiness or the deepest despair.".

Loose lips sink ships, so it's crucial that the words you say to yourself and about yourself are indicative of what you want in and for your life. Pay attention. Be mindful of your mouth. Stop instructing yourself in self-destructive ways!
Speak of your successes in the making, the many fine attributes you have, and your nearly untapped abilities to make things happen. Merely because you might not see them doesn't mean they don't exist. You've simply kept yourself so blinded that you've lost sight of them.

PAY ATTENTION to what you're saying and thinking to yourself. Be intentional with words and make the intention POSITIVE. Negate the negativity!
If you catch yourself, correct it.
No need to berate yourself further.

Overwhelm the messages of the world and in your own negative self-talk with positive messages to and of yourself.
Never downplay the miracle that is you; uphold how amazing you are and learn to control the directive.

Last, but not least.

"What goes into someone's mouth does not defile them,
**but what comes out of their mouth,
that is what defiles them**."

Jesus Christ: @ Matthew 15:11

Thoughts to ponder:
What do I tell myself about myself?
What do I say to myself that isn't what I want?
What are the "I always this" or "I always that" comments that I make to myself and others – as well as the remarks that say how I can't, how I never, and how nothing I do will change, make a difference, or matter?

Notes:

SLEEP... it's about Time

I'm putting this out there now because I didn't want another night to go by for you where either too much or not enough sleep was contributing to your propensity to make excuses instead of making things happen in your life.

We all know someone who burns the candle at both ends, professing that they will "sleep when they're dead".
This one hits home with me, because there was a challenging time in my life where I was trying to exist on 2 hours of sleep a day, and I did this for almost a year. I don't recommend this unless your goal is to impair your health and risk permanent damage to your body and brain.
What I DO recommend is that you invest the time to determine how much sleep is optimum for you to function at your best without sacrificing time you'll never get back.
Most of us have heard we need a good 8 hours of sleep.

Like most things, there are exceptions to the rules.
History is heavily peppered with famous and successful people who slept well below the "required" 8 hours of sleep.
For example:

Nikola Tesla, Thomas Jefferson – 2hrs
Isaac Newton, Donald Trump, Dwayne Johnson – 3-5hrs
Florence Nightingale, Martha Stewart, Margaret Thatcher, Voltaire, Napoleon Bonaparte - 4hrs
Winston Churchill, Jay Leno, Thomas Edison - 5hrs
Alexander Graham Bell – 4-6hrs
Richard Branson, Kelly Ripa, Elon Musk - 5-6hrs
Arnold Schwarzenegger - 6hrs

There are also numerous people who seem to require *more* than the daily recommended 8 hours of sleep. What matters most is finding out how much sleep YOU need. Something that you may find of interest is that the effects of not enough sleep is very similar to that of excessive sleep. So, if you think that you can live longer and experience great health by sleeping all of the time – guess again. Extremes of either are detrimental.

One thing you'll note is that the people mentioned on the list of examples have been very successful in various ways. What you'll find they share is that they were willing to do in common hours the uncommon things that most people are unwilling to do. Sleep is one thing that most successful people admit to sacrificing at times in order to get ahead.
What I don't want you to get out of that is that sleep loss equates to success. Don't let your mind play tricks on you.
To put it bluntly, staying up late at night spending one's precious time in mindless activities is no recipe for success.
Quite the opposite, because it steals away the energy and acuity you need to recognize and seize the opportunities that abound and surround you during the day.

Since we're on the topic of sleep and the hours we devote to it – consider that our time is a resource. It is a commodity we trade and barter every day, and each of us is allotted 24 hours a day to invest, spend, or waste. As I said earlier, when it comes to the life we want, it we will find it as a result of the uncommon that we are willing to participate in – not the common and average. I heard it said in my early twenties that successful people are willing to do what unsuccessful people are unwilling to do and will have as a result what others will not. I never took that to mean success strictly in the financial realm, but in all areas of life. Creating the life we want in every area takes intention and devotion no matter what the distractions are. Invest your time wisely where it will bring you abundance in return. In your family, in your finances, in your passions and purpose – these are all areas that typically fade to a mere acceptable status quo if left unattended.

Time is the biggest excuse that comes up as a "reason" for not being able to pursue what they want – and it's widely accepted as valid and true. At the same time, all of us have "killing time" activities that drain away precious hours of our lifetime, paying no dividends nor interest toward the life we say we want.
What if you had a checkbook for your time?
At 12am midnight $1,440 is deposited into your account - $1 for every minute of your life. If you went to bed at 10pm and woke up at 6am, write out a check for $480 and toss it under the pillow. Write out a $60 check for the hour it took to get ready and eat breakfast.
If you're keeping track, we're down to $900 – and we haven't even left the house. When you get into the car, stuff another $60 check into the glovebox for your to and from work travel.
At work, there are many checks to write.

$15 should cover going through your irrelevant emails,
with a $10 check to cover a conversation with a coworker that
had nothing to do with work. A $120 check should cover various
social media interaction throughout the day, which might sound
steep, but I'm sure it was worth it. Another $30-$60 check
should cover your lunch. More checks for projects,
conversations, bathroom breaks, etc.
By the time you get home from work you'll find you've written
checks for about $540... and you're down to $180.
Don't forget to lay a check for $60 under your dinner plate.
It's 8pm, and you've got $120 left to spend on your family,
hobbies, extracurricular activities, passions – minus a
$15 check to cover getting ready for bed expenses.
Before you know it, you're out of $time$.

I have an idea – stop writing bad checks!
Seriously, if you had to write a check at the end of any activity,
interaction, conversation, etc. – wouldn't you be far more likely
to weigh the importance of it and evaluate its worth VS the cost?

Make your minutes count and you'll find you have far more time
available to you than you realized, and invest it wisely.
People make time for the things that matter,
 and for the rest – they make excuses.

Treat your time as the precious commodity it is,
and expect others to know it's worth also.
If you treat your time carelessly, so will others.
If you don't respect your time, neither will they.

Not enough time is no excuse to never start;
it is a reason to press forward to the finish.

Be uncommon in the common hours –
willing to do and be what the unwilling won't
 - and you will have a life that they cannot.

Notes:

Places where time is spent without regard to cost:

What would I do with an extra hour every day?

Who do I allow to dictate how I spend my time?

Is what I am doing now the best use of my time, talent, and abilities to create the Future I say I want?

Which came first -
The emotion or the motion?
(Does it matter?)

As a child, my mother would sometimes tell me that she was going to tie my hands behind my back because (apparently) I would talk with my hands a lot.
It turns out, as research would show, that it's a sign of higher intelligence when children frequently talk with their hands.
I'm running with that one, of course. What's even more interesting and relevant in my case is that my using hand gestures was more than likely compensating for the challenges I had in verbal communication. Talking has never been my strong suit, that's why you're reading this book instead of listening to me share in some other format.
I know you've heard the term "body language" before, more than likely in the context of something you're doing that's communicating how you're feeling. Often, we don't even think about it. Yawning when we're bored is an obvious one. Biting or digging at our fingernails when we're nervous or anxious is another. Rubbing your chin when you're deep in contemplation is common. Frowning indicates you're probably displeased.
So, let's broaden the scope, shall we?
After all - what's this have to do with making excuses??

Answer:
your state of being.
If you're in a lousy state of being and have a poor frame of mind - the likelihood of you making excuses is many times higher than if you were in a state of joy, happiness, peace, optimism, and other such positive and productive "moods".

Allow your body to communicate a message to the brain
that will snap it out of its "L" for Loser state
and whip it into a "V" for Victory!

Most people would equate body language to (in summary) an external physical reaction / expression to what's going on internally / emotionally.
In essence, your mind is communicating to and commanding your body to respond to it, as a response to the thoughts, emotions, and feelings it is experiencing.
Your emotions will elicit motion automatically.

Right. OK. So...
We've spent a lifetime with these physical responses reflecting our internal experience, yet have done very little with the reverse effectiveness. Most people have lived their lives at the mercy of their emotions, believing them to be beyond their control. As most of us know, being logical and "thinking" away emotions by trying to be rational only goes so far.
Besides, who, under the reign of their emotions, has that kind of will power or ability to think clearly? Very few.
I'm not saying that emotions do not serve a purpose, because they absolutely do, and I'm not talking about repressing them. What I am sharing is that we can interrupt the rule that they too often have over our life. Especially for those whose emotions overwhelm them and consume their time, energy, and ability to move forward and toward those things that that would better serve them; having a way to regain control over themselves would be a long overdue blessing.

I heard Zig Ziglar say many years ago;
"*Logic* will not change an emotion... But **action will**."
You could probably look at many examples in your own life.
At times you may have had a million reasons to do something, it made sense to do it, and you knew you should do it, and there was no good reason at all why you shouldn't do it -
BUT YOU DIDN'T **FEEL** LIKE DOING IT... So, you didn't.
Even though "I don't feel like it" seems like a weak excuse at best, time and time again it's been shown that most people make changes and take action based far more on what they feel – **not** what they know.

Now, for those of you who have ever uttered "I can't help how I feel", first of all STOP saying it because you're further programming your subconscious to make it true for you! Instead, let's look deeper into this two-way street of mind/body connection and how you can make it work for you.

There are expressions and gestures that are fairly universal among people, as well as those that are more individual.
One of the most valuable observations you will make in your life is **OF** your life; *how you are within your life*.

If you aren't aware of how you react to your feelings, emotions, and ways of being - pay attention.
In your victories, in your tragedies; when you feel love, when you feel hate - What is your body doing?
What are the expressions and gestures that come through?
Knowing what these automatic reactions are can become an invaluable tool for you.

For example, when we're sad or depressed - we tend to close ourselves up, slouch, and withdraw, or in grief and pain we might even curl or wrap ourselves up, as if to protect.
Have you at times found yourself feeling sad or depressed, and not really knowing why? Check yourself.
What is your position and posture?
How are you holding yourself and your space?
Often when you put your body in resemblance to the reaction of a feeling or emotion, you will begin to elicit and experience those emotions and feelings that would typically precede those actions.

If you find yourself feeling uninspired, lazy, or lethargic - check yourself. You're probably slouching and not moving your body much, if at all. Your head is most likely held low, and your face probably looks the part - wearing a frown; your lips together, corners turned down. If you want to prolong feeling sad, down or depressed - laying around is one way to keep these emotions in play by allowing your body's posture to continue sending "reminder" signals that you must be sad, down, or depressed. Science and psychology have long supported that one of the easiest ways to shift out of a depressed state is through action and mobility, while a sure way to prolong it is through immobility and inaction. Over a period of time, what might have begun as a short-term response to a given situation is often recorded as a standard way of being. This can be incredibly detrimental to those whose lifestyle is more sedentary and lacking in activity. Because their inaction, which IS a physical act, reflects the same positions and postures as those that are reactive to depressive states, those feelings and emotions that are experienced in that state are often brought forward. With these feelings and emotions now present, the response to them is further initiated, and the cycle continues; action creating emotion, emotion causing reaction, reaction (in this case further inaction and withdrawal) eliciting emotion, and so forth.

Now, let's move to the other end of the spectrum.
We've all heard the saying "Chin up!", declared
usually by others who are trying to cheer us up.
Though I doubt that the origin began in science, the resulting benefits provide further evidence that by adjusting our physical state we can alter what we are feeling. Many of you are probably familiar with the quote by William James;
"*I do not sing because I am happy - I am happy because I sing*".
I've always enjoyed whistling, and when I heard that quote at the age of 22, it stuck with me. I never "got" the connection when I was a kid, but I didn't need to understand it; the results were present regardless. Whistling impacted my emotions.
I recently saw a video clip where a basketball player had missed a shot and was seen walking away with his head held down, shoulders drooped forward - looking quite defeated. Another player quickly ran over and physically lifted his head up (chin up!). In that instant you could see the man's posture shift and his countenance change from one of looking defeated to one that reflected determination and confidence.
I'm not certain if it was for the sake of appearance or for the attitude adjustment - but it worked regardless. (Tip there).

Watch what people do (physically) when they win, when they succeed and triumph in a situation, or achieve a goal.
Look at what they're initial gestures, movements and physiology is. Oftentimes these motions are reactionary to the moment - a reflex of the emotion they're feeling inside.

In your own life, pay attention to your body's reaction;
When you're excited
When you're happy
When you're confident
When you're in control
When you're winning
When you're at peace
When you're calm

As you may suspect, when it comes to the excuses you make, they're usually not coming from a place of empowerment. Typically, they are made when you feel like you're not in control, not capable, not confident, and in a fear-based mindset.
Always be mindful of your presence and the position of your body that it isn't negatively affecting your presence of mind in the matter - because it will if you're not paying attention.

If you've found you've slipped into some posture that doesn't have you in a positive mindset, adjust yourself.
Check your self before you wreck yourself!
Chin up! Sit or stand up straight. Shoulders back. Breathe deeply, grateful for the air that now floods your lungs, and appreciative for the lymphatic system that you are stimulating. Smile at how silly a notion it is that you can alter how you feel by how you move. Smile even bigger
as you begin to realize that it does and is.
Test the other ways that you might affect how you're feeling - even try throwing your arms above your head like you just crossed the finish line of the New York marathon in first place, or like Rocky Balboa on the steps of the Philadelphia art museum.
(You have seen the movie "Rocky", right? Talk about a movie that didn't allow excuses to get in the way of conception, inception and production!)

ACTION can break you out of the prison of disempowerment that negative feelings and emotions all too often create.

When you don't FEEL like doing anything positive, productive, meaningful, or beneficial toward your goals or in your life - most of the time, you won't. It takes a serious amount of discipline to dig in and plow ahead with what you know you need to do.
Of course, sometimes just digging in and taking action, *regardless* of how you feel about it and despite whether you want to or not, *will* be enough to begin shifting how you feel. Mankind has been aware of this for centuries.
Still, wouldn't it be nice to begin with a positive mindset - motivated and inspired - excited and wired?
SPOILER ALERT: Y E S. It *is*.
Additionally, beginning in this way of being will get you to think in ways of how you CAN accomplish what you're up to instead of wasting your creativity making excuses.
Put yourself in positions that are empowering.
Move your body in ways that are motivating
and your mind will shift from telling you what
you can't do to finding ways that you can do.

Notes:

MORE Notes:

Before I move on, I'm going to suggest something.
Get excited about life; more specifically - *YOUR life*.
If you can't, at least start acting like it until you are.
After all, who else is?
And until YOU ARE excited about your life
 - same question; Who else is going to be?!?

Look around.
Aren't we all just a little too stuffy and reserved?
It's as if it's cool to act cool, indifferent, apathetic, and nonchalant about things. "It is what it is" we say, and move about our day - never moving beyond to "What *could* it be?"
We've been so brainwashed and led to think that the accepted way to be in society is to act laid-back, stoic, and borderline apathetic in our life and appearance to others.
In so behaving, *we are creating this very mindset of being*.
It's no wonder multitudes of people live so impassively and create such uneventful lives.
God forbid we actually show that we care about things - that anything really matters to us; that we might actually have a pulse and passion for life and what it has to offer.

I don't mean this to be a revelation,
but I'd love it to be a wake up call.

**Every second of your life that goes by
is one less second you have to live.**

You're somewhere in between birth and death,
so that means there's still time to get on track to
having a life that you ARE excited to live every day.

It doesn't matter what your yesterdays looked like,
*and the longer you look there to validate your present -
the longer it will take you to create the life you really want.*
Being fixated on the past only pushes it further into your future.

Update. Current events: Pandemic, panic, and pandemonium.

We have before us the opportunity of a lifetime; a chance to look at what we might create within a life so shaken out of the norm.

Most of us have done the familiar in Life.
We know what to expect day to day - for better or worse, good or bad; it is what we have come to expect.
Into this familiarity we recognize our resources, our abilities, opportunities, and limitations.

And now... our "normal" is anything but.
We've been forced to be mindful of how we interact with the world. Our patterns have been broken up - habits, schedules, and routines shredded. So much of what we've taken for granted has suddenly shown us its value and its cost.

If you've ever wanted an excuse to make dramatic and powerful changes in your life - this could be the launching pad you didn't know you were waiting for.
You're already shifting the usual in your world.
Your status quo and normal way of being has been interrupted, disrupted, and otherwise corrupted.

Instead of trying to swim back upstream hoping things will get back to "normal" again; why not push the envelope of your potential and pursue those hopes, dreams, and passions that required you to step out of your comfort zone?

The world needs you to be extraordinary -
which means it's time to get rid of the ordinary and
give up your illusions and delusions of inadequacy.
They've never served you - only enslaved you
to the comfortable life you've settled for.

Your decisions and direction don't need to be popular,
and you don't need permission for your mission.
No matter what your circumstance or situation,
now is the time to be bold and present to possibility.
In the shadow of the unknown, resist the urge to cower.
That is the all too familiar reaction - that is what you know.
Move instead in faith, with courage, and conquer it.

**Stop settling for the life you see;
make it the one you want it to be...**

Do you know what a hamster calls its cage?

Home.

I want you to think about that for a moment.

Within that confine, it learns
where it can and can't go -
what it can and can't do.
It eats and drinks what is given it,
plays with whatever objects it finds,
runs and runs on its little hamster wheel,
and that... that is Life. Every. Day. Life.

I doubt that it ever considers that this Home Sweet Home
is actually a contraption built to limit its level of freedom,
rather than a fortress protecting it from the outside world
- sheltering it from the dangers of the great Unknown.

I want to bring another form of movement to the forefront,
and more than anything it has to do with our movement in life;
the moves and motions of our everyday living within our world.

We are habitual Beings - creatures of habit we've been told -
made complete by the routines that serve as reminders of who
we are. Many of us become confused and out of sorts if familiar
things are not present or certain rituals performed.
To move forward and become more than you currently are,
you must break the created habit of your Being as you know it.

Do you want to have each day a repeat of the day before?
Just follow the automatic routines and patterns that you've been
doing every day, each one an anchor to the unremarkable - a
reminder of life being un-extraordinary.
You're setting your mind on cruise control - to experience
and engage with the familiar and expect nothing more
than refracted and reflected versions of the day before.
Regardless of the change in scenery of opportunities -
you're stuck seeing the re-runs of episodes gone by.

Even with the most magnificent orchestra in the world at your command, you conduct "Chopsticks" because it's the one you know the best - and tomorrow's performance will be as stunning as todays.
Bravo.
You're a Ferrari Testarossa convincing and creating yourself to be a Ford Pinto from the time you wake up to the time you fall asleep. You go through your day acting like it and achieving it wonderfully, thanks to a mind and body combination beyond our comprehension and vastly underestimated in power.

Over the years, some of the more common messages shared through many forms of media have been that if we want to keep our brains sharp, we should challenge them every day.
Although it is great that there is a growing mainstream awareness of the decline of our cognitive function, all too often it's often blamed on aging. Of course, age can play a role, yet to the extent it is experienced and throughout the actual age groups it can be traced – cognitive decline and impedance are far more a result of environmental impact and influence.
Again, this is one of those rather inconvenient truths I'd rather not get too sidetracked on. The subject of environmental impact and influence on the mind and body is the main topic of one of my other works. For now, the acknowledgement that our minds are affected by the external is sufficient, and this much we've already touched on earlier.

Back to sharpening our brains!
The 2 things I've heard for a number of years now that always stuck out for me as things we could do to help keep our wits about us were doing crossword puzzles and taking a different way to work. Now, crossword puzzles have never appealed to me, but taking a different way to work seemed doable.
It always *seemed* like a good idea, but I rarely tried it. Too many good excuses not to, like "I'm running late" or "I might get lost" or "I'll do it tomorrow when I'm not so pressed for time".
I'd recycle my excuses over & over, too, so I'd never have to be too hard-pressed to invent new ones.
You may have similar examples.

The point is, one of our "rut" creators is driving to work the same way day after day. That advice of taking a different way to work is deeper than I'll bet anyone intended it to be.
You're not just sharpening your mind
 - you're breaking up patterns.

Have you ever shaved, brushed your teeth, or applied lipstick with your left hand if you're right-handed – and vice versa? How about putting your keys in a different pocket?
It feels strange, unusual, odd, and weird... at first.
Try backing your car into your parking spot if you always pull in straight. Pull in straight if you usually back in.
Whichever you feel compelled to do, switch it.

If you're employed, what if you took on that you weren't an employee at your job. What if you started the business of You and agreed to take on a familiar client in your new business? Go for a test drive in a car that is out of your belief to own, and when you hand the keys over, tell the salesman
 "You can borrow it for now, but I want a full tank of gas when you bring it back. And don't forget to wash it!".
How about taking a drive through neighborhoods you'd like to live in? Wave at people walking and remind them what day trash pick-up is, just like they were your actual neighbors.

This may sound ridiculous and slightly bizarre. Consciously.
Your subconscious, however, doesn't have that sense of humor. It's seeing what is, and hearing what's said.
Not only is this breaking up your normal way of being,
but it's planting the seeds of a reality you want as if it were.

Remember what we touched on earlier
about *our mind not being able to differentiate between what is real and that which is vividly imagined?*
Recall also that bringing what we want to a place of ownership and familiarity in the present will cause our subconscious to work overtime toward making it (or rather KEEPING it) so.

If you keep going down the same familiar roads of your life, you'll keep creating the same ruts in your life - in all areas.

Break up the normal of your life.
Stop duplicating the days gone by and
start painting the life you want in the here and now.

Understand the power of being in the present -
of not reliving and repeating the familiarity of the past.

Every day holds opportunities and obstacles, and your ability to discern and determine one from the other grows daily - allowing you to learn from the known and unknown alike.

By being intentional with your self and in your world you can begin tapping the potential of what you're really capable of - not what you've come to expect.

By being aware of how you're *being* in body and mind, and positioning both to places that would better serve you - you will operate at optimum levels of creativity and action.

Instead of the usual excuses for not doing things, you will - in ways beyond comprehension - find yourself moving forward in a state of positive expectation and confidence. Whatever your results in the moment will not be viewed as failure or success, but merely steps in a desired outcome.

Let me repeat that in a shorter version:

Your results in the moment are steps toward a desired outcome.

The most exciting aspect of all of this is that it will lead to and eventually evolve into your new way of Being - both in your level of Awareness as well as your reaction and course of action to and in Life.

Considerations and Notes:

What meaning are you assigning the results you get?
_____
_____
_____
_____
_____
_____
_____
_____
_____
_____
_____
_____
_____
_____

It's good that we ended the last section mentioning awareness, because I felt there needed to be an appropriate segue (pronounced "segway" in parts of Italy) for this next subject. Now that we have it, I can tell you that we're switching gears a bit - because we know that's one of the ways that we're going to break out of the old habits that have been the expectation and creation of You, right?

I'd like to introduce you to a few people, or should I say traits, that might seem... familiar.
You and I both know people who seem to live a life riddled with various forms of drama, for lack of a better word. It shows up in their family and relationships, their work, politics, recreation - you name it. There always seems to be some some kind of struggle found in various areas of their lives. For them, continuous complaint and corruption abounds, and the excuses never end. (I won't bore you with a long list of examples, so this is the one time I'll let you off the hook for skipping ahead.)

(Examples START HERE)
It can look like a job where they have to work with people who don't know what they're doing, or that friend who jumps from relationship to relationship when the intoxication of a "new" person wears off. For another, a high rate of infidelity can be their "fix". Promiscuity is also a related and common rush - the thrill of the chase to the unchaste. Volatile relationships are another common way people keep drama in play.
Many people thrive on making others angry or upset, engaging in various ways of poking and prodding to produce reaction. These types often disagree for the sake of disagreement and argue for the sake of arguing. Mention politics or religion to these types and prepare for the eruption of corruption. Competitiveness, both the participation of directly or indirectly (think sports, for example), can also fit the bill.
(Examples STOP HERE)

Now, the tricky part in all of this is that these behaviors and ways of being occur as more or less "normal" for these people. It's just how life is. It's just how they are. To tell them different oftentimes is to invite defensiveness, denial, deflection, justification, and yes - you guessed it; Excuses.

"That's just the way I am" is the absolution and ultimate defense for those who, like the hamster, consider their cage "Home".

Having established this, what has so many of us drawn to this way of life - this accepted, adapted, and desired level of normalcy? Glad you asked!

In a nutshell, in spite of what's right and despite what's wrong, we tend to do what feels good - and what feels good is all in your head. The "How" is primarily through the release of chemicals in the brain. Of course, given our tendencies to go with what we know, if we know that engaging in dramatic scenarios will result in a payoff (a chemical fix) we'll keep doing it. Why stop, right?

The full answer to that involves more conscious payoff/cost equations - a conversation to have once our awareness of them is present. For now, let's go with the more prevalent unknown and unaware state of being we're in when we do what we do without really knowing why.

The examples are endless, yet what they have in common is the ability to, on some level and to varying degrees, stir and stimulate stress responses.

In these moments, especially more extreme ones, the pulse doesn't just increase; it pounds. Your breathing quickens, flooding your body with additional oxygen and nutrients.

Your level of awareness and alertness is also increased, as is your energy level, and even your sense of inspiration and motivation can be elevated.

You might be wondering at this point "What's the downside?" So far, this all sounds good. Exciting even!

Yet it gets better. Within and at the conclusion of these onsets, if there is a "win" or victory to be had and we're left having been vindicated, justified, or our sense of being right established - additional chemicals are introduced into the brain that make us feel good. The same chemicals that are responsible for us feeling pleasure, joy, happiness, and elation are released.

Again... Not really seeing a downside to this, are we?

That is, until we consider that not only are we taxing our bodies ability to produce these chemicals in the first place, but we're creating a type of addiction to them. And, as most addictions, they require more and more of the "drug" to bring about the same result, which further taxes the body & brain.

A number of these chemicals that are continually spiked into the system can lead to health conditions such as diabetes, increased weight, heart disease, memory loss, depression, vitamin deficiencies, and even cancer, to name a few. Unfortunately, the long-term debilitating effects will often not be realized until it is too late to do anything about them.

Additionally, we're also "hardwiring" these typically negative scenarios with the reward centers of our brain. End result, and without even knowing we're doing it, we will find ourselves in situations where drama is present. We will create it. To us it won't look like it - it will look more like we just happen to find ourselves in dramatic situations. We will also typically have a number of people in our lives the same way, which feeds and stimulates this inner craving for both ourselves and for them. For example, these things are often present for these people:

Something is wrong / There is a problem
Something isn't right /Something isn't fair
They need to be right / They need to make it right
They crave attention / They have to be noticed
They have to win / If they don't win, it's wrong
 - and the list repeats.

Time to ask the question again - How does this tie into excuses?

Because your excuses are often a tool to include or create drama in your life, and it doesn't take long before drama is a part of your life and a welcome part of your comfort zone.

Your subconscious will be the enabler to your brain's "addiction" and find ways to create drama no matter how wonderful your circumstances are or how well your situation in life is.

Now, I should have mentioned this earlier, and I would be remiss if I didn't also mention these under the category of "Ways To Keep Drama in Play".

How many people do you know who just HAVE to watch their TV show? More than likely it's a show that includes some amount of drama. Why do you think "reality" shows are popular?

Have you ever seen people who can't put your phone down for 5 minutes? They have to get that text, see that message, scroll their feed like the social media junkie it's designed to create.

For the record, social media = top tool for creating drama and feeding it since the invention of television. Hands down.
In all its many forms, it's all candy to the brain, and the sweet tooth it has will keep growing unless you break the cycle and reset the head.

So how can we unhook ourselves from the highs and habits we've unknowingly become addicted to?

Regain the brain and refrain from falling into poor habits.

First of all, if you find yourself slouching or slumping - fix it. Create the habit of maintaining a productive posture, then go the next step of positioning and moving your body in ways that will make you feel a more positive and empowered state.

If you're feeling anxious, nervous, or worried - long, deep breaths will help stimulate chemicals that bring you calm and peace, whereas rapid, shorter breaths will have you feeling more energized if you're lethargic, uninspired, and unmotivated.
Use your breathing as a tool to achieve the state you want to be in. One place to gain instruction for both positive movement and breathing is through yoga. Do your due diligence, though, and don't assume any yogi in leotards or spandex knows how to intentionally shift the brain with breathing and movement of the body. It would also help to give up preconceived notions and stereotypes around the word "yoga".

If your current solution is reaching for a pill or pushing some product into your face every time you feel "off", STOP. I realize this could be a big challenge for many. We've been sold on the idea that it's normal to pop a pill, toke on some smoke, drink half a pot of coffee, pop open an energy drink, and numerous other popular means of artificially taking us from the mood of the moment to where we hope to be.
The mind is a master chemist, and is constantly creating elixirs that can heal, and also those that will bring you harm.
Newsflash:
Your body is designed to give you everything you need - we were simply born without an advanced User Guide on how to program and operate it at optimum levels for maximum performance. Our "default" was set early in our development, and we've been on cruise control ever since - making excuses to others and ourselves as to why we are the way we are,
why we are where we are, and Who we are in life.

If you will build the habit of being aware of how you are feeling and what your state of Being is, you can train yourself to automatically posture your body into positions that empower you, and likewise bring mindfulness to the type of breathing that would serve you best in the moment. You will also have the cognition to recognize the surrounding factors and forces that may be negatively influencing you and take proactive steps to limit them. When your mind and body are in tune to making the most out of your abilities and discovering resources available, excuses do not exist.

Now, earlier I alluded to the tug-o-war of trying to keep this book short by not inundating you with too much "how" and "why" detail, all without shortchanging you in the process. The subject of brain chemistry is enormous, as is its influence and importance to the operation of the mind and body. Anything that impacts, alters or otherwise affects it can change our world as we know it, to which we are reminded again:

*"Though we are fearfully and wonderfully made -
our workings are fragile and susceptible to influence."*

What we know about the brain - it's function, composition, and operation - is incredible; mind blowing in every sense. Even more inspiring is what we have yet to discover.

The good news is that we don't have to know it all before we can make meaningful changes in our life. Understanding key concepts and applying them, rather than being debilitated by the overwhelm of details, is what will lead to you gaining control over your life.

<u>Reminder:</u>

Many in the field of human development say that people change because of emotions and feelings more than we do based on reason and fact.

With this in mind (literally), and knowing that feelings and emotions are chemical compositions controlled in the brain, we can be intentional with the tools that would stimulate the mental soup that makes us FEEL good, positive, and right about doing something, taking action, and making changes.

*"Though we are fearfully and wonderfully made -
our workings are fragile and susceptible to influence."*

What can you do to strengthen the condition and composite of your mind and body, while being mindful of the influence and control that YOU have access to in and over your life?

What you write here can change your Life:

What are you *willing* to do to strengthen the condition and composite of your mind and body, *being mindful to the influence and control that YOU have access to in and over your life?*

<u>**What you write here *WILL* change your Life:**</u>

What resistance do you have, if any, to strengthening the condition and composite of your mind and body, or toward the certainty that you have influence and control over your life?

How do you rank?
Who and How you are in your World

If you're game for discovering something about yourself that may be just outside your own scope of view, try this:
Interview people close to you who are quite different than you. Get their feedback on how they see you operate in the world. You can simply tell them that you are working on an assignment in Self-Awareness, and let them know that you already know there are many things you don't see about yourself (that's why you're doing the assignment!) and that you expect and are prepared to hear even the toughest news. Give them free reign to be completely honest - that's what you need, without the sugar coating usually shared among friends. For the sake of this topic, be sure to ask them if they've heard you make any excuses that surprised them... and any that didn't.

Regardless of what they share, DON'T shoot the messenger! This is also not the time to be argumentative, justifying, or try to explain away anything that is brought up. You're not on trial. Keep in mind that you won't likely see the same patterns or be paying attention to your way of being. Remember - your life, however it may look on the outside, occurs fairly normal to you - just as the lives of other people seem pretty normal to them. Often, those on the outside can see what you might be blind to and even offer an insight and perspective you may not be aware of. This means nothing less about you as a person; quite the contrary. A wise person knows they don't know everything, and that includes everything about themselves.

Let me mention again that these people you interview should be quite different than you. The reason for this is primarily because someone a lot like you will likely also have similar views as you, as well as levels of awareness. They will tend to see what you see. Though it's nice to gain agreement with people,
we're looking for growth - not gratification.
Our blind spots are more apt to be seen by others of a different view, from another perspective other than our own, and what is seen from there can be quite eye opening and revealing.

Which brings me to this very relevant point that I'm sure you've heard many times before; *"Birds of a feather flock together."*

As you would suspect, associating with others who have "like" ways of being will further trigger and stimulate your own.
If many of your friends are dramatic, that stimulates your own tendency to feed on drama. That being said, whatever those things that you are, for lack of a better word, "addicted" to - your familiar and similar "flock" is playing a part in keeping you stuck. They may trigger your drama drip more than you know.
You will tend to mirror and mimic over time those who you spend time with, and even take on the emotions they present with as a result depending on your innate level of empathy.
If your circles of association include people of similar nature who do things and engage in similar activities as you do, they may unknowingly be enabling your appetite for brain candy.
Be intent with whom you surround yourself - not simply content.
They can be your greatest support to lift you up,
or an unwary opposition that pulls you down.
Choose those who are encouraging, uplifting, and
will help hold you accountable to your word with yourself.

An example of how this may look would be if you come up with an excuse that isn't in alignment with what you say you want, a positive association will bring it to your attention and show you that it's just that; an excuse. A negative association will agree with you and the excuse you made, and try to make you feel good, justified, and "right" about it.
Now, I hate to be the bearer of bad news in a society that seems to increasingly cater to and coddle feelings as more important than fact - but doing everything because it "feels good" is often deceptive and destructive in the long run.
Remember - your subconscious is trying to keep you in a comfort zone. Therefore, it is going to give you "feel good" feelings to keep you making decisions and choices that keep you stuck, and make things feel difficult to lure you away from opportunities that would have you leave the nest of perceived security (your comfort zone).

Now, if you've established your underlying belief system to operate under the premise that you are worthy, deserving, and owning the life you truly desire (in progress), then you may consider "trusting your gut" more.
Just be aware that, until you reach that point,
trusting your gut will often lead to getting more of
what you've already got and believe that you deserve.

Time for a tidbit of more practical application.
Regarding the flock you fly in.
A major segment of the population spends a majority of their waking hours in a position of employment in a workplace outside of their home more than anywhere else of influence. This means that the people with whom you "flock" there are affecting you, like it or not. If they are negative, it affects you negatively.
In reality, polluting the environment with sounds that are negative (in music and speech, for example), affects everyone - including the source. This may not be a popular notion or subject to bring up, because few people want to think that they are wrong or that what they like (or their way of being) is bad or detrimental in some way. They tend to take it personally, and an attack on things they like is an attack on them in their eyes.
Still, don't think it's beyond your control or out of your level of influence if you aren't the "boss". That's your excuse talking. You'd be amazed at what a mature conversation about what negatively impacts the individual can do for people - especially people who understand that as each person is more empowered, they will be more productive and therefore more profitable.
A good manager appreciates and has an open mind to ideas and suggestions that are beneficial, even if they did not come up with them on their own. That's how the best leaders become the best; by being open to and welcoming ideas from others that might be outside of their own scope or view.
If they aren't at a level to understand that - what a great opportunity for YOU to make a difference in your workplace and professional environment! They might even thank you for it.

Lesson:

Choose wisely those who you spend time with and create opportunities to see yourself from an outside perspective.
Be a positive influence among the people around you no matter who they are or their role and create a more positive environment for everyone as a result.

Resistance to this and any associated excuses are the groans of your comfort zone wanting you to go back to sleep, not wake up and succeed.

*Though we are fearfully and wonderfully made -
our workings are fragile and susceptible to influence.*

Empowering ideas, Resistant thoughts, and other Notes:

Final thoughts, recapped & uncorked.

For the record - "I don't know how" IS an excuse.
It's one of the most popular, yet ridiculously weak.

Common sense says
that everything you know
you never knew before you knew it,
and it's not exactly earth-shattering news
that you don't know what you don't know -
or even that you don't know that you don't know it.
Wrap your head around that for a few moments.

Just appreciate and never overlook that ALL OF US
are given the opportunity to learn new things every day,
and never underestimate how powerful the results
can be when opportunity and preparedness meet.

The tools to being prepared are in your hands -
the opportunities are already within reach,
waiting to be unveiled and revealed.

That Thing you want, yet don't know how to get.
The Where you want to go, but don't know the path.
The Who you want to be, yet can't seem to become.
The What you want to accomplish, but haven't achieved.

So, you "tried" it once and you "failed". Really?
Change your tactic. Reframe the "failure".

What actually happened:
~ You put in an action and achieved a result.

Congratulations!
You're on the right track. Bravo.

If it wasn't the result you were hoping for,
change the action you put in, or where you put it.
Be mindful that the results of your endeavors could lead to the
discovery of something that might be useful and beneficial to the
end result - IF the end result is truly what you seek.

Release the attachments you have as to *how* the
path should look on the way to what you want.
Don't let pride keep you from the prize, and
don't allow stubbornness to steal your success.

When you experience "failure", ask yourself;

  What do I *believe* about what happened
  that might be preventing me from *seeing*
  all that actually happened?

Is my conclusion based on reality
or a biased reflection of my own
expectations and past experiences?

Have I put anything into the space that would
delude my being open to all possibilities?

What meaning have I given to what happened?

Earl Nightingale stated it succinctly;
"Whatever we plant in our subconscious mind
and nourish with repetition and emotion
will one day become a reality."

With the floodgates of negativity open in society,
more than ever it is crucial to guard against toxic
messages that would assault our eyes and ears.
Be mindful of the manipulation and the motives
behind what we are given to see and hear.

Every day is an opportunity to develop education,
and you will have learned something by nightfall -
either by what you've chosen to be taught,
or allowed in without conscious thought.

Garbage in, Garbage out; Value in, Value out.
Your brain is a treasure - Stop filling it with trash!

Overwhelm the demeaning messages of the world and in your
own negative self-talk with positive messages to and of yourself.
Never downplay the miracle that is you; uphold how amazing
you are and learn to control the directive.

Remember - the subconscious mind doesn't distinguish
between what is real and that which is vividly imagined.
Push back against the negative narratives you see and hear.

Hold in your mind first what you seek to hold in your hand.

Go beyond imagining it; experience it as accomplished.
See yourself in ownership of what you want -
engage all of your senses to know and feel its presence.
In crystal clear clarity, allow your mind to absorb that the life
you are living IS comprised of your various dreams, goals, and
desires - ALREADY obtained; as real as the ground at your feet.

While you're planting the positive in your mind,
don't neglect what you're placing in the body.
A strong body supports a strong mind,
just as a strong mind will support the body.

Weakness of the body will have your mind convince you to take
the easy way in to and out of things that may not be in your
best (conscious) interest, using excuse after excuse for your
conscious to agree with. When you lack proper health, your
mind can make you feel lethargic, lazy, unmotivated, and even
ill - with any number of these being used as excuses every day.
Again - this is for your protection, courtesy of the subconscious;
it doesn't want you to compromise health any further by
exerting more effort than is necessary.

Be moved in your Being by being moved in body.
Learn to be present to your placement
and mindful to the motions of your body.
Study the movements that trip and trigger your emotions.
Develop those postures and positions that put you in a positive
state of mind and support feelings of control and empowerment.
Break yourself from being a slave to excuses like "I don't feel
like it" and master those maneuvers that would shift you to
feeling energized, confident, and unstoppable.

With regard to those who share the world with us,
we would be wise to be intent, not merely content,
with whom we surround ourselves with.
They can be our greatest support to help lift us up,
or an unwary opposition that pulls us down.
Choose those who are encouraging, uplifting, and
will hold you accountable to your word with yourself.
They can also help bring attention to excuses
that might slip under your conscious radar.

...and remember
it's not where you start in the race, but WHEN.
Your past is nothing tangible, nor to be used as
some repetitious handicap that holds you back.
The past is merely the time passed before you got to NOW, and
now is the best place to start making your life extraordinary.

It's time to stop the making of excuses
for and from the Life you can have,
and never again leave your living
to some default status of circumstance.

The End ~

        of who you were -

                the beginning of realizing

                        who you are.

I'd like to bring your attention to something that,
if you were to grasp the significance of and embrace it,
would likely be almost overwhelming to be with.

Regardless of your beliefs, faith, or lack thereof -
consider these words regarding mankind, a.k.a. You and me.

"For thou hast made him a little lower than the angels,
  and hast crowned him with glory and honour."
                                          Psalm 8:5

"I praise you, for I am fearfully and wonderfully made.
Wonderful are your works; my soul knows it very well."
                                          Psalm 139:14

"And God said,
Let us make man in our image, after our likeness:
and let them have dominion over the fish of the sea, and over
the fowl of the air, and over the cattle, and over all the earth,
and over every creeping thing that creepeth upon the earth… "
                                          Genesis 1:26,27

"You have made him a little lower than the angels;
   You have crowned him with glory and honor,
   And set him over the works of Your hands."
                                          Hebrews 2:7

What if you actually believed these statements?

*Consider that they are true
regardless of your belief.*

It could be incredibly enlightening and transforming.

~Robert H. Steffen

Made in the USA
Monee, IL
27 November 2020